HOME TRUTHS?

TECHNOLOGIES OF THE IMAGINATION NEW MEDIA IN EVERYDAY LIFE
Ellen Seiter and Mimi Ito, Series Editors

This book series showcases the best ethnographic research today on engagement with digital and convergent media. Taking up in-depth portraits of different aspects of living and growing up in a media-saturated era, the series takes an innovative approach to the genre of the ethnographic monograph. Through detailed case studies, the books explore practices at the forefront of media change through vivid description analyzed in relation to social, cultural, and historical context. New media practice is embedded in the routines, rituals, and institutions—both public and domestic—of everyday life. The books portray both average and exceptional practices but all grounded in a descriptive frame that renders even exotic practices understandable. Rather than taking media content or technology as determining, the books focus on the productive dimensions of everyday media practice, particularly of children and youth. The emphasis is on how specific communities make meanings in their engagement with convergent media in the context of everyday life, focusing on how media is a site of agency rather than passivity. This ethnographic approach means that the subject matter is accessible and engaging for a curious layperson, as well as providing rich empirical material for an interdisciplinary scholarly community examining new media.

Ellen Seiter is Professor of Critical Studies and Stephen K. Nenno Chair in Television Studies, School of Cinematic Arts, University of Southern California. Her many publications include *The Internet Playground: Children's Access, Entertainment, and Mis-Education; Television and New Media Audiences;* and *Sold Separately: Children and Parents in Consumer Culture.*

Mimi Ito is Research Scientist, Department of Informatics, University of California, Irvine, and Visiting Associate Professor at the Graduate School of Media and Governance of Keio University, Kanagawa, Japan. She has published widely on new media and youth and led a recently completed three-year project, Kids' Informal Learning with Digital Media, an ethnographic study of digital youth funded by the MacArthur Foundation.

DIGITALCULTUREBOOKS is an imprint of the University of Michigan Press and the Scholarly Publishing Office of the University of Michigan Library dedicated to publishing innovative and accessible work exploring new media and their impact on society, culture, and scholarly communication.

Home Truths?

VIDEO PRODUCTION
AND DOMESTIC LIFE

David Buckingham,
Rebekah Willett, and Maria Pini

The University of Michigan Press and
The University of Michigan Library
Ann Arbor

Published in the United States of America by
The University of Michigan Press and
The University of Michigan Library
Manufactured in the United States of America
♾ Printed on acid-free paper

2014   2013   2012   2011   4   3   2   1

A CIP catalog record for this book is available from the British Library.

Library of Congress Cataloging-in-Publication Data

Buckingham, David, 1954–
    Home truths? : video production and domestic life /
David Buckingham, Rebekah Willett, and Maria Pini.
        p. cm. — (Technologies of the imagination series)
    Includes bibliographical references and index.
    ISBN 978-0-472-07137-1 (cloth : alk. paper) —
    ISBN 978-0-472-05137-3 (pbk. : alk. paper)
    1. Video recordings—Production and direction.
    2. Video recordings—Social aspects. 3. Video recording.
    I. Willett, Rebekah. II. Pini, Maria, 1965– III. Title.
    PN1992.94.B82   2011
    384.55'8—dc22   2010033749

Dedicated to Albie Fiore

Acknowledgments

The research reported in this book was conducted as part of a three-year project entitled "Camcorder Cultures: Media Technology and Everyday Creativity" (2005–8), based at the Institute of Education, London University. We are very grateful to the United Kingdom's Arts and Humanities Research Council for its support.

The authors all worked on the project over this period. David Buckingham is director of the Centre for the Study of Children, Youth and Media at the Institute of Education. Rebekah Willett is a lecturer in education, specializing in media, children, and education, and is also based at the Centre. Maria Pini was a researcher on the project.

We would like to express our thanks to many people who have assisted us in different ways: our colleagues Shakuntala Banaji, Liesbeth de Block, Andrew Burn, Diane Carr, Sue Cranmer, and John Potter for their input on the project; Ryan Martinez, our student intern, for the hours he spent at the computer; Richard Diehl, Andy Hain, Colin McCormick (the Web masters of www.labguysworld.com, www.totalrewind.org, www.colin99 .co.uk), and Jerome Monahan for their help with the historical section; and above all, our participants for welcoming us into their homes, giving us access to their videos, and sharing their thoughts and experiences.

Contents

Introduction

Since the first domestic video cameras were introduced on the market almost a quarter of a century ago, the opportunities for ordinary people to create their own moving-image representations have steadily grown. In the United States today, around 45 percent of households own video camcorders, while in the United Kingdom (where the research reported in this book was conducted), the figure is around one-third. The advent of mobile (cell) phones with video recording capacities and the "bundling" of digital editing software with standard home computers have led to video making becoming significantly more accessible, even ubiquitous. Meanwhile, YouTube and similar sites have made it much easier for people to share and distribute video to both known and previously unknown audiences.

Yet despite its increasing scale, there has been very little academic research on this phenomenon. This book arises from what we believe is the first large-scale social research project to explore domestic and amateur video production. Our research, which took place between 2005 and 2008, covered two main aspects. First, we looked at a series of amateur video making communities, ranging from skateboarders to amateur pornographers, and from groups of young men creating "spoofs" to share online to well-established clubs of elderly film and video makers. These were "serious amateurs," for whom video making was a sustained leisure-time pursuit involving sometimes considerable investments of time and money. In addition to an online survey, we conducted a series of in-depth case studies, using interviews and observations, as well as viewing a large number of amateur video productions. We have published our account of these "camcorder cultures" elsewhere (Buckingham and Willett 2009).

While they are interesting to study, such amateur groups are obviously unrepresentative. Very few of the millions of people who now own video cameras are likely to engage in video making in such sustained and dedicated ways. In most cases, the camera is likely to be used only occasionally, perhaps on special occasions, or simply when the opportunity arises. For much of the time, it may languish unused in the cupboard or under the bed. In the terms provided by the sociologist Robert Stebbins (2007), most domestic video making is more a matter of "casual leisure" than "serious leisure": it is intermittent, spontaneous, even haphazard, rather than being a committed and regular practice.

In most cases, these everyday uses are also likely to be confined to what Richard Chalfen (1987) calls the "home mode"—that is, the use of media to represent the private world of domestic life. Here, we find people recording children's birthday parties, family outings, and holidays or simply fooling around, playing with the camera. These people are not primarily interested in video making as an activity in itself: they may not care much about the quality or the aesthetic character of what they produce or about the technological potentialities of their equipment. They may well be concerned to capture events as clearly and even accurately as they can, but they are not particularly interested in improving their camera technique, editing their recordings, or showing their videos to a wider audience beyond family and friends. On the contrary, their interest is essentially in the *content* of what they record and in the possibility that video affords of being able to view that content again, perhaps at some point in the future when the people and places they have captured are only distant memories.

It was with the aim of exploring these more everyday practices that we undertook the second part of our research. Via a local school and a community center, we recruited a group of 12 households living in the vicinity of our university research lab in central London. This was a very diverse group, in terms of social class, family composition, and ethnic background. We gave each household a video camcorder to keep and tracked what they did with it over a period of around 15 months. This was clearly not intended to be a representative sample, but an in-depth, broadly "ethnographic" collection of case studies. We visited and interviewed members of each household on several occasions and gathered examples of the videos they were making. What the participants did with their video cameras was very diverse, and by no means was all of it confined within the home mode. In addition to the birthday parties, holiday footage, and playful messing about that we expected to find, we also gathered and were told about examples of video diaries, documentaries, comedy skits, and remakes or parodies of well-known films—as well as a great deal of material that defies easy categorization or indeed interpretation. This book is the result of our analysis of all the data we collected.

As we write, there is growing excitement both in academic circles and in public debate about the democratic potential of new media technologies, including digital video. We are apparently moving into a new era of "participatory culture," in which power is passing away from the elites and multinational corporations that used to control the media and into the hands of ordinary people (for more and less cautious examples of this argument, see, respectively, Jenkins 2006 and Hannon, Bradwell, and Tims 2008). While we certainly sympathize with the aspirations that are often expressed here, we are very skeptical of the more grandiose claims about the impending democratization of media. There are various reasons for this. While some of these are beyond the scope of this book (see Buckingham 2010), the key issue that concerns us here has to do with the unrepresentative nature of the practices such enthusiasts tend to describe.

In this as in many other areas, cultural studies researchers are often keen to fix on areas of cultural activity that appear somehow subversive, radical, or challenging. Henry Jenkins's (2006) work on "convergence culture," for example, focuses largely on highly dedicated groups of media fans, who are busily appropriating and reworking existing media texts through their own creative media productions. This is fair enough, but as Jean Burgess (2006) argues, it may lead us to neglect the more banal, everyday ways in which people use media—which in the case of video making are typically much less cool and glamorous. Just as enthusiastic fans cannot stand in for media users in general, so dedicated amateurs do not represent "ordinary" people's use of video.

Cultural studies frequently proclaims its interest in "popular representation," but it has tended to ignore or marginalize the very forms of popular representation (and indeed *self*-representation) in which "the people" are routinely engaged. As we shall see in chapter 1, there has been some useful work on domestic photography, but very little sustained analysis of home movie or video making. In our view, researchers need to resist the continuing temptation to look elsewhere for the really cool stuff and spend more time engaging with the kinds of mundane, everyday cultural practices that we consider here.

In the following chapter, we provide a broad context for our discussion of home video making and discuss some of the theoretical perspectives and the previous research that have informed our work. We set the scene by considering the widespread dissemination of domestic video technology and the ways in which home video making is discursively "framed" in both popular and academic commentary. In general, we suggest, the home mode has been viewed pejoratively, as somehow insufficiently serious, artistic, or indeed politically challenging. We outline some academic perspectives that might enable us to understand what ordinary people do with video in a less dismissive and judgmental way.

Chapter 2 gives an account of the methodology of our project and introduces the 12 households that we studied. We draw attention here to some of the methodological and ethical issues raised by this kind of broadly "ethnographic" research and some of the dilemmas and choices that we faced in analyzing and writing up our data.

Chapters 3, 4, and 5 then present our analysis of the data. Rather than discussing each household in turn—an approach that we find leads to rather laborious reading—we have sought to pull out some broader themes that cut across our individual case studies. We recognize that this may place greater demands on the reader's attention—rather like reading one of those nineteenth-century novels with an enormous cast of characters—and so we hope that readers will be able to refer back to the brief introductory sketches we provide in chapter 2.

In chapter 3 we provide an overview of the range of video making practices in the 12 households. We describe the different reasons and motivations for video making, the ways in which the technology was used, and how the participants defined their identities as video makers. Our main focus here is on the ways in which video making was accommodated within the texture of everyday domestic life: where and when people used the camcorder; who in the household was able to use it and for what purposes; and how this related to broader divisions of power within the family (e.g., in relation to gender and generation), as well as to wider networks of extended family and friends. The discussion in this chapter thus relates to broader debates about the sociology of family life and specifically to recent work on the "domestication" of technology.

Chapter 4 focuses on the subjective experience of video making and its place in relation to emotion, memory, and personal identity. It begins by considering how people respond to the experience of seeing themselves on screen and, conversely, how it feels to be the video maker. It then moves on to look more broadly at the role of video making in relation to memory and the creation of "narratives of the self." It explores how our participants used video as a means of freezing passing time for future viewing, how this future was imagined, and how video enabled them to create stories of their lives and to locate themselves in their physical and emotional world. This chapter builds upon theories of identity and subjectivity, including psychoanalysis, which have previously been used in relation to still imagery (notably domestic photography).

In chapter 5, we look more closely at how and what people learn about video production. We explore the different methods that our participants used to learn—for example, referring to published sources, seeking help from others, learning by doing, and imitating or drawing on mainstream media models. We consider the extent to which they planned their videotaping, whether they edited or engaged in other "post-production" activities, and what motivated them to want to make "better" videos. We then move on to look at *what* they learned—their understanding of the specific qualities of video as a medium, their awareness of "film language" and specific techniques (e.g., to do with framing and editing), and the different aesthetic and generic sources and traditions on which they drew. This chapter thus relates directly to contemporary discussions of "media literacy" and to broader theories of learning.

In our conclusion, we turn to what we suspect is the key question that will be nagging many of our readers. What is the social, cultural, and political significance of such apparently mundane activities? Is widespread access to "the means of media production" likely to precipitate a revolution that will overthrow dominant forms of media power? And if it is not, then what purpose and value does it have? Here, we want to contest the sense of *disappointment* that pervades much academic discussion of home video making—the sense that some potential challenge to the Powers That Be has somehow been defused or recuperated and that people have been distracted by trivialities. This is of course a familiar argument in discussions of popular culture, and in this context, it is accentuated by a view of the home mode as somehow necessarily conservative and supportive of a particular "familial ideology." We hope that our analysis of these 12 households will provide a more nuanced and sympathetic account that does better justice to the contingencies of ordinary people's everyday lives and the diverse roles that media play within them.

CHAPTER I

Understanding Home Video

Media representations of home video making tend to portray it as a rather comical, even somewhat ludicrous, practice. Typical scenarios involve earnest fathers carefully staging "spontaneous" performances by their bored and reluctant children, friends and neighbors being lulled to sleep by endless screenings of family holiday films, or teenagers misguidedly emulating the dangerous stunts on TV shows like *Jackass*. The films themselves are generally deemed uninteresting, unimaginative, and unwatchable. At best, perhaps, enthusiasts might hope to capture some of the pratfalls and bloopers routinely featured on *America's Funniest Home Videos* or the United Kingdom's *You've Been Framed*—albeit with the wobbly camera work, poor framing, and uneven focus that are seen as indispensable characteristics of the genre. But is home video making simply an infinite wilderness of domestic trivia? Is it merely the last refuge of the annoyingly proud parent, the obsessive hobbyist, or the teenager vainly seeking to become the next Steven Spielberg? And in the face of these apparently obvious limitations, why do people obstinately persist in wanting to record their children's birthday parties and holidays or in capturing hours of footage of family and friends waving and mugging for the camera?

In this chapter, we provide some pointers toward a less dismissive account of home video making. We review previous research on home movies, family photography, and home video, and we consider some of the broader claims that have been made about the significance—or indeed, insignificance—of such popular representational practices. Some of the research we address here is taken up in more detail in our discussion of our own data in chapters 3, 4, and 5. To begin, however, we need briefly to set home video making within a historical context and to consider how this practice is framed and defined within the commercial market.

TRACKING BACK

Although our research focuses on video making at the beginning of the twenty-first century, amateur movie making has a long history, dating back to the early 1900s. Indeed, many of the key landmarks of early cinema—like those in the early history of photography—were produced by "gentlemen amateurs," mostly wealthy middle-class men with sufficient time and resources to dedicate to what was essentially a hobby. "Home movies" became more widely available with the development of the 16 mm Cine Kodak and Kodascope Projector in 1923. The camera weighed about seven pounds and had to be hand cranked at two turns per second during filming. It cost $335 (by comparison, a new Ford car could be bought for $550). The first major period of home movie making began after 1932, when Kodak developed the Cine Kodak Eight, which used 16 mm film but only exposed half the film at a time, enabling double use. Other manufacturers emulated Kodak, with Bell and Howell developing the Filmo Straight Eight camera, which carried 8 mm film only. In 1936 Kodachrome color film was developed to meet the ongoing boom in home cinematography, even though the equipment and film costs were still prohibitively expensive for most. World War II halted major technical advancements for the domestic film market, and it was not until the 1960s that technological changes created significant opportunities for those interested in home movie making.

With the launch in 1965 of Kodak's Super 8, an easy-load cartridge system that ran through the camera once, filming was made easier, while at the same time cheap plastic cameras were reducing the cost of home movie production. The 1960s also saw the advent of video, which allowed the filmmaker to watch a production back immediately, without having to send it away for expensive developing. In 1963, the Neiman Marcus Christmas catalog included the Ampex "home video" system, which included a large camera (weighing 100 pounds), TV monitor, and video recorder, all costing about $30,000 (including home installation). The first affordable portable video recording system was released by Sony in 1965—although its affordability and portability are certainly arguable. Aimed partly at recording programs from television, Sony's CV-2000 "videocorder" weighed 66 pounds, videotaped in black and white, and cost $695 plus $40 for each one-hour reel of tape. The camera kit, which weighed 20 pounds, could be purchased for an additional $350, for a total of $1,085, including one tape. (Calculations based on the consumer price index indicate that with inflation, this would equate to over $7,000 in 2009.)

In 1967, the Sony DV-2400 Video Rover emerged as the first truly portable video recording system. According to the Sony product literature, "The Battery Operated Videocorder, in a comfortable, compact shoulder-pack, weighs a mere 11 pounds!" (SMECC n.d.). The Rover, or portapak, required separate playback equipment, had a maximum recording time of 20 minutes, and cost $1,250 (equivalent to over $8,000 in 2009). Panasonic and JVC followed soon after with their own portable models, eventually reducing the weight of the entire pack to 30 pounds.

In the 1970s, portapaks were mainly used by news agencies, as well as countercultural movements and avant-garde artists such as Nam June Paik. However, by the mid-1970s, home video making was becoming more economically viable, partly due to the introduction of domestic VCRs and the development of inexpensive half-inch videotape cassettes (with two main formats emerging, Sony's Betamax in 1975 and JVC's VHS in 1976). Sales in film cameras dropped dramatically with the introduction of cameras that could be attached to VCRs, although until the early 1980s, video making required separate camera and VCR devices. In 1982, Sony introduced a professional camera, the Betacam, which was both a *cam*era and a re*corder* (or camcorder). This first camcorder was used primarily by news agencies, as the Betacam videotape recorder cost up to 100 times the price of a consumer VHS machine. In 1983, Sony released the first camcorder for domestic consumers, the Betamovie BMC-100, weighing just 5.5 pounds and costing $1,500 (equivalent to $3,230 in 2009). Sony's advertisements claimed:

Simply pop in a standard Beta cassette and you're ready to shoot continuously for up to 3 hours and 35 minutes. Without carrying an awkward separate recorder. Without getting tangled in wires and cables. And without being weighted down by heavy equipment. . . . Betamovie takes all the trouble out of making home movies and gives you all the fun. (Total Rewind n.d.).

In just two years, from 1981 to 1983, home movie production shot up, with 6 percent of U.S. households reporting owning a video camcorder in 1981 and 28 percent in 1983 (Chalfen 1987). During this time, JVC developed the compact VHS format (VHS-C), which was designed for more portable VHS players and was eventually used in the first JVC camcorder in 1984, the GR-C1. In 1985, Amstrad developed the first low-budget camcorder, the VMC100, which cost $400 (equivalent to $800 in 2009) and weighed just under 2 pounds. Cheap and simple camcorders were even developed for children as early as 1987, with the Fisher-Price PXL-2000, priced at $99 ($187 in 2009) (LabGuy's World n.d.).

In spite of these developments, camcorders were still significant financial investments for the average household. Issue One of the United Kingdom's *Camcorder User* magazine (Spring 1988) listed the average selling prices of a camcorder as around £1,100 ($2,035, equivalent to about $3,700 in 2009). Numerous advertisements in this issue offered 0 percent finance deals for camcorder purchases, and one article discussed negotiating with sellers to have a two- to four-day trial period, describing the purchase of a camcorder as "an awesome task" that "can be a very frustrating experience . . . and a very costly one if you make a mistake!" (Hi-Spek Electronics 1988). Clearly, camcorders were not yet for the average consumer.

The next significant technological breakthrough was in 1995, when the first digital camcorders were introduced. More than 50 companies had agreed on a DV tape format the previous year, and these first camcorders released in 1995 were aimed at professionals. In 1996, the digital camcorder hit the amateur market with miniDV tapes that allowed transfer to computer hard drives via Firewire or USB. This would lead to various digital formats, including Digital8, DVD, micromv, hard drive, and solid-state (flash) semiconductor memory. In combination with Firewire technology, "bundled as standard" digital editing software on home computers brought sophisticated and good-quality filmmaking and editing within reach of ordinary people.

In 2000, video-related sales in the United States grew by 15 percent, with total sales of $3.3 billion. Prices continued to drop: from 2001 through 2005, the average unit price fell from $423 to $319 (Consumer Electronics Association 2006). In 2005, disposable camcorders were available for just $30 (plus a $12 processing fee). Camcorder sales rose 11 percent to 5.9 million units in 2007 and were forecast to rise another 4 percent in 2008 to 6.16 million (Consumer Electronics Association 2008).

The turn of the century also brought video to other platforms such as mobile (cell) phones and still cameras. In 2000, the first mobile phones with built-in cameras were launched, followed shortly by the development of phones with built-in video recording facilities and large memory cards. By 2004, camera and video came as standard on new mobile phones, and in 2007, 87 percent of camera phone owners reported using the camera function on their phone (PMA Foresight 2008).

The distribution of video footage was radically transformed with the emergence of free video sharing sites, particularly YouTube, which was launched in December 2005. YouTube was an instant success: during its public preview the month before the official launch, cofounder Chad Hurley claimed that YouTube was moving "8 terabytes of data per day through the YouTube community—the equivalent of moving one Blockbuster store a day over the Internet" (Market Wire 2005)—although clearly much of this material was not produced by amateurs. Numerous video sharing sites followed, some of which promised to distribute advertising revenue to contributors, and Google ultimately bought YouTube for $1.65 billion in October 2006, less than a year after its original launch (Geist 2006). News stories suggest that in January 2008 alone, "nearly 79 million viewers, or a third of all online viewers in the US, watched more than three billion user-posted videos on YouTube" (Yen 2008), while the number of videos on the site is rapidly approaching one hundred million.

These technological developments have undoubtedly made video production available to far more people. At present, video comes standard with mobile (cell) phones, costing as little as $50, as well as with many digital still cameras. Camcorders (with memory cards) cost as little as $90 and weigh less than 0.25 pounds (compared with the very first $1,500 camcorder, equivalent to $3,230 in 2009, which weighed 5.5 pounds), while the Flip camcorder, which plugs directly into a computer (without a wire), is the size and weight of a small digital still camera and costs around $100. Yet with the availability of video facilities on so many different platforms, it is difficult to assess current levels of video making. While the technology is undoubtedly *available* to more and more people, questions remain about whether more videos actually *are* being made; who is making them and for what purpose; and whether different kinds of things are being videotaped, edited, and distributed than was the case in earlier decades. Video appears to be ubiquitous, to the point where it has become a taken-for-granted aspect of everyday life for many people, yet there has been relatively little systematic analysis of what this entails or, indeed, of its consequences.

FRAMING THE HOME VIDEO CONSUMER

Anyone who uses—or even considers purchasing—a video camera is bound to encounter a large amount of advice of different kinds. Family members, friends, and salespeople are likely to offer more or less helpful suggestions, but beyond personal contact, there is a whole world of advice literature in the form of manufacturers' publicity materials, handbooks, consumer and hobby magazines, television programs, and Web sites aimed both at novices and more experienced users. Such material typically offers quite prescriptive ideas about what to film, where to film, who to film, and how to film. While it is certainly diverse, it all serves to define and construct the *meaning* of amateur video making in particular ways.

Elsewhere, we have undertaken an extensive analysis of the discursive construction of amateur film and video making within books, manuals, consumer magazines, and other material, dating from 1921 to the present day (Buckingham, Pini, and Willett 2007). While much of this material is implicitly targeted at the "serious amateur" or hobbyist rather than the casual user, it generally assumes that "personal," family-oriented films are likely to dominate. Thus, in his introduction to *Amateur Cinematography,* published in 1962, Bordwell writes of amateur films:

These films are a faithful record of our lives. Big events and small have been telescoped into a few vivid moments, which we can experience again as often as we wish. Intimate family reunions or crowded public meetings; the back garden or a panorama of woods and mountains; scenes from childhood, from holidays at home and abroad—it's all there, only needing the projector to bring it to life. (13)

Likewise, in Kodak's *How to Make Good Home Movies,* written in 1966, the authors assert, "Most [film-camera] owners are not at all interested in using their cameras for subjects other than purely personal films of family and friends" (Kodak 1966, 5). Throughout the 1970s and 1980s, the home mode continues to be identified as the central function of amateur film and video making. Alan Cleave (1988), for example, provides a typical list of subjects for filming, including weddings, family holidays, sports events, and children's birthday parties; and the same categories routinely recur in subsequent handbooks and manuals. More recently, Steven Beal's *Complete Idiot's Guide to Making Home Videos* acknowledges that

many people buy camcorders for one reason: to document their children's lives as they grow up. . . . Never before in human history have we been able to record and document with such accuracy the most important events in our lives. (2000, 203)

This emphasis on the home mode, or at least on the private and personal nature of video making, is also strongly apparent in marketing pitches. A Sony advertisement from 1991, for example, attempts to entice younger consumers to buy smaller camcorders for their holidays:

Something happens between the milestones. Between the weddings and the birthday parties. It's called the rest of your life. (quoted in Baum 1991)

A similar emphasis is apparent in a more recent example from 2007:

Your trip to Paris. Your child's first steps. College graduation. Life is full of moments that are well worth remembering. There's no better way to capture those moments than with a Sony Handycam® camcorder. (Sony Electronics 2007)

Even so, the material we have analyzed is also concerned with distinguishing between the *serious amateur,* the enthusiast who invests in technology and creates "artistic" finished products, and the *everyday user,* who owns relatively inexpensive technology (with no accessories) and does not plan or edit his or her films. Everyday users are typically identified with the home mode in its crudest and most unreconstructed form: their video cameras are used simply for keeping "records" of family life. By contrast, most of the books and consumer magazines are addressed to readers who are aspiring to move (or are in the process of moving) from being everyday users to becoming more committed amateurs and hence have an interest in improving their practice (and in investing in more expensive equipment). It is through the process of "othering" the everyday users that this key distinction is created and sustained: it is always *others* who are uncreative, who do not plan their filming, and who bore their audiences with poorly shot, unedited family movies.

Thus, even when it comes to making "family films," readers of these manuals and magazines are repeatedly urged to be more adventurous and creative. For the serious amateur, the making of such films is more than simply a matter of neutral record keeping. In order to create an accurate picture, the filmmaker must plan carefully so as to capture "typical" actions rather than random events. Readers are urged to analyze professional filmmaking practices, learning and applying "film grammar" and techniques (such as the "rule of thirds," the "180 degree rule," and continuity editing), as well as paying close attention to camera angles, lighting, storyboarding, and scripting. Editing is consistently identified as a defining characteristic of "good" amateur filmmaking. Amateurs are repeatedly encouraged to cut out irrelevant shots and to be ruthless about discarding film that does not progress the narrative: the aim is to create films that are more interesting for audiences and, like commercial films, tell a story. Although realism is consistently held up as the preferred aesthetic of amateur film, considerable attention is paid to the ways in which filmmakers need to shape and construct events in order to create the illusion of realism and spontaneity. Readers are urged to cut out shots that show people hesitating, "acting up," or looking directly at the camera.

The discourses of these publicity and advice materials clearly show the continuing importance of the home mode, but they also reflect a broadly dismissive attitude toward it. The serious amateurs at whom they are targeted are implicitly conferred with a degree of creativity and social distinction that differentiates them from the naive or untutored home video maker. Nevertheless, as Richard Chalfen (1987) points out, the rules and injunctions contained in such texts are almost entirely at odds with what the large majority of home movie makers actually produce: even if they are aware of such aspects of "good" filmmaking (as they are surely likely to be from their own everyday consumption), they nevertheless fail to apply them to their own productions. Likewise, as we shall see in chapter 5, hardly any of our participants consulted such texts in seeking to learn more about video making, and indeed, few of them were sufficiently bothered to attempt to emulate "professional" (or even "serious amateur") standards. This was not, we would argue, because of ignorance or laziness: it merely reflects their rather different aims and motivations.

MEDIA IN THE HOME MODE

To what extent do these constructions of home movie making in advice literature and consumer publications coincide with the findings of academic research? Unfortunately, research studies in this field have been conspicuous by their absence. Recent research on the everyday use of media in the home has focused almost exclusively on people's activities as "consumers" rather than as producers. There is quite a long history of research on families' uses of television (e.g., Morley 1986; Lull 1990), although in recent years much of this work has concentrated on information and communication technologies (e.g., Berker et al. 2006; Haddon 2004; Lally 2002; Silverstone and Hirsch 1992). This research focuses on the "domestication" of technology—that is, on the ways in which it is appropriated and incorporated into the fabric of domestic life. It considers how the use of technology changes over time, how it relates to the dynamics and power relationships within the household, and how it varies according to the values or "moral economy" of the family. More recent research has pointed to the flexibility of these processes and to the fact that the boundaries between the home and the wider world may be fluid and porous (e.g., Bakardjieva 2006).

This research usefully cautions against deterministic ideas about the "effects" of technology on family life and linear notions of how technological innovations are diffused within society. We take up some of these ideas in more detail in chapter 3. However, it should be noted that this research remains strangely focused on *equipment*. While there is some discussion of what people *do* with equipment, or the content that they access through it, these things often appear only as examples: the focus is typically on the television, the computer, or the mobile phone as a medium in its own right. Furthermore, these studies rarely refer to people's creative or productive uses of media, even in the case of home computers, and studies of domestic photography, filmmaking, or video making are few and far between.

One of the most useful starting points here remains Richard Chalfen's account of domestic photography and filmmaking, *Snapshot Versions of Life* (1987), which is based on material gathered from middle-class U.S. families during the 1960s and 1970s. Chalfen's analysis of the home mode is essentially anthropological: he is interested in domestic media making as an everyday symbolic practice and in uncovering the implicit social norms on which it is based. He provides a useful analytical method that focuses, for example, on the different roles that people take up when making home movies; what, when, and how they choose to film; what counts as a "good" shot or sequence; and how the resulting footage is edited, manipulated, and exhibited. (We take up this approach in relation to our data in chapter 3.) The focus here, then, is on the rules and conventions that govern the social practice of media making, rather than on its psychological significance for the individual.

As we have noted, Chalfen finds that there is a complete contrast between the prescriptions offered in "How To Do It" manuals about photography and home movie making and what people actually do in practice. Thus, people rarely plan or edit their films, they pan and zoom wildly in their efforts to capture events, and they show people posing or "acting up" rather than behaving naturally. Home movies typically focus on a very narrow spectrum of the available subjects: they avoid banal or potentially taboo areas in favor of predictable footage of vacations; special family events; or shots of people posing, waving, or simply staring at the camera. Likewise, snapshot photographs tend to feature carefully chosen moments in the life course that show progress or development—the child's first steps, the award of a school diploma, rites of passage, and family vacations: there are no disasters, illnesses, or problems, and very few mundane everyday events.

Chalfen sees this kind of amateur media making as a means for individuals to construct their own visual histories and thereby also to feel that their lives are coherent and meaningful (an aspect that we consider in more detail in chapter 4). These represented histories are clearly partial and selective, even if people tend to regard them as truthful documentary "records": they follow socially expected parameters and thereby reaffirm particular values or forms of cultural membership.

This cultural or ideological dimension is emphasized more strongly in Patricia Zimmerman's history of amateur filmmaking in the United States, *Reel Families* (1995). However, Zimmerman takes a much less sanguine view than Chalfen: indeed, she argues that the increasing focus on the home mode that emerged during the early decades of the twentieth century effectively reduced amateur filmmaking to a trivial, privatized leisure pursuit. According to Zimmerman, this "domestication" of amateur production defused its radical democratic potential and its ability to address social or political issues: it became "an atrophied, impotent plaything, a toy to endlessly replay repressive ideologies" (142).

Even so, Zimmerman's history suggests that this was a gradual and uneven process. In the early part of the century, the boundary between amateurs and professionals was somewhat blurred. The amateur was seen to enjoy a degree of freedom from commercial imperatives, and hence a degree of creativity, that was less available to the professional, although this was typically manifested in a specific amateur aesthetic of "pictorialism" that was carried over from still photography and painting. However, from the 1910s to the 1950s, the innovative potential of amateur filmmaking was steadily channeled into a narrow focus on the nuclear family. Instructional books and popular magazines persistently "directed amateurs toward creating a narrative spectacle of idealized family life"

(Zimmerman 1995, 46). By the 1950s, Zimmerman suggests, the "famil-ial" ideology was effectively triumphant: filmmaking was defined as an affirmation—even a celebration—of the blissful domain of the (nuclear) family home.

Zimmerman argues that this ideological construction of amateur film in publications and marketing was reinforced by industry practices. She traces the ways in which the industry maintained barriers to entry for amateurs, for example, by standardizing distinctions between amateur and professional gauges of film (16 mm versus 35 mm, and subsequently 8 mm versus 16 mm). In the 1950s, the market became more differenti-ated, as further distinctions emerged between domestic consumers and more serious hobbyists, although the key boundary between amateurs and professionals was strongly sustained.

Similar arguments have been made about the "amateurization" of still photography (Burgess 2007; Slater 1991). On the one hand, Kodak's mechanized system of photographic processing—"you press the button, we do the rest"—made possible the mass popular use of the medium, but it also constrained the possibilities for experimentation and inno-vation, both technically and aesthetically. As Slater (1991) argues, the representations of the family in Kodak's marketing materials also tie in with the emergence of mass consumer culture: family photography is steered toward idealized images of children and holidays that have much in common with those in mainstream advertising. As we shall argue in more detail below, such apparent "democratization" of access to media production does not necessarily result in significant changes in existing structures of power and authority.

Zimmerman's history focuses primarily on the public discourses and commercial practices that sought to define the proper place of the ama-teur filmmaker, rather than on actual films themselves. The few specific examples of amateur film she describes are not so much "family films" as travelogues drawn from museum archives and produced by dedicated amateur anthropologists (several of whom, interestingly, are women). Indeed, one of the problems of this kind of historical work is that it is almost bound to rely on material deposited in archives, which is by definition rather untypical. Similar arguments could be made in relation to other historical studies of amateur filmmaking, in both the United

Kingdom (e.g., Norris Nicholson 1997, 2001) and the United States (e.g., Stone and Streible 2003).

The histories provided by such authors generally conclude before the advent of video, although both Chalfen and Zimmerman do discuss the possible implications of this new technology in their closing pages. James Moran's *There's No Place Like Home Video* (2002) remains the only book-length study of domestic video production, although it remains curiously evasive when it comes to discussing what people actually do with their video cameras. As Moran suggests, there have been significant shifts since the advent of video, not just in technology but also in the nature of family life. Although he is keen to avoid overgeneralizing about the specific qualities of the medium, Moran argues that the affordability of video as compared with film, and its facility for instant recording, replaying, and erasing of footage, may well result in greater quantities of material being produced—and thus perhaps in less selective representations of family life than those identified by Chalfen. Meanwhile, changing family structures have undermined many of the assumptions of the "familialism" Zimmerman describes and potentially led to greater diversity in representations of the domestic sphere. Jose van Dijck (2005) goes further, arguing that home video has fundamentally subverted the idealized images of the family contained in home movies and on mainstream television: the realism of video, he suggests, is "a weapon in the struggle for emancipation." According to van Dijck, digital technologies accentuate this further: the possibilities of better-quality, easier editing and distribution of material "appear to give the individual amateur more autonomy and power over a more complex, (multi)mediated portrayal" that is more attuned to "contemporary, fractured notions of family and individuality" (33). While such claims may seem overstated, they do suggest that the home mode has continued to evolve historically in light of changes in both technology and family life.

Moran (2002) makes a strong case for the home mode, arguing that (unlike high culture) it "affirms a sense of continuity between life and art" (xix). He is strongly critical of Zimmerman's argument about the ideological recuperation of amateur production, suggesting that it is based on a kind of political elitism, and he also challenges, on similar grounds, those who have celebrated the "radical" use of home mode footage in the work of avant-garde filmmakers such as Maya Deren and Stan Brakhage. Like Chalfen, Moran asserts the positive functions of home mode production: it is "an authentic, active mode of media production for representing everyday life"; "a liminal space in which practitioners may explore and negotiate the conflicting demands of their public, communal, and private, personal identities." It helps to articulate generational continuities, communicate family legends and stories, and establish the role of the home as a "cognitive and affective foundation situating our place in the world" (59–61). Nevertheless, Moran seems strangely reluctant to discuss any actual examples of home mode video or of the people who make it. The focus of his empirical work is not on home video, but on semiprofessional "event videography" (in the form of wedding and memorial videos), which he accuses of somehow colonizing authentic home mode production; he discusses at even greater length the use of home-video-style material in commercial movies and television shows (from sitcoms like *The Wonder Years* and *Ozzie and Harriet* to independent or art movies such as *Sex, Lies and Videotape* and *Family Viewing*). By default, this approach defines home video in terms of what it is not: it represents an imagined authenticity—as compared with the variously inauthentic ways in which it is used or misused—but it is not explored in its own right.

PRIVATE PRACTICES

There are some parallels between these discussions of amateur film and video making and research on amateur photography—although here again there have been relatively few substantial academic studies. Here too, the ideological significance of the home mode—or, in this instance, the "family album"—has been equally contested.

Susan Sontag's (1977) well-known critique pauses briefly on the relationship between photography and the family, although her targets are more wide-ranging. Photography in general is indicted here for condoning moral superficiality, regressive nostalgia, predatory voyeurism, and other forms of "mental pollution," and while Sontag's most scathing observations are reserved for "concerned" photojournalism, she also notes how the use of photography within the family functions as a "social rite, a defense against anxiety, and a tool of power" (8). Like Zimmerman, Sontag regards the popularization of photography not as a means of democratization, but as a way of shoring up the "claustrophobic unit" of the nuclear family in a social climate of growing insecurity.

Critical accounts of photography typically dismiss family photography as little more than an endless repetition of the same story: the happy, unified, stable family narrative. Pierre Bourdieu (Bourdieu et al. 1990), for example, argues that "ordinary practice seems determined to strip photography of its power to disconcert" (76). As Gillian Rose (2003) puts it, there is general agreement within studies of family photography that "family photos are stifling in the limited possibilities they offer for self-representation" (6). Families are shown as happy, at leisure, integrated, and safe. "Otherness," conflict, tension, and difference are all erased in favor of images of sameness and cohesiveness. In Don Slater's (1995) words, family photographs are "generally regarded as a great wasteland of trite and banal self-representation(s)" (134).

This argument has been taken up, but also challenged, in a tradition of critical feminist work on family photography that dates back to the 1970s and 1980s. On one level, the family album is seen here as a source of sanitized images of happiness and togetherness that gloss over and repress the conflicts and inequalities of power that are actually central to family life. As Holland (1991) argues, family photography attempts to reassure us of the solidity and cohesion of the family at precisely the point where it is becoming fragmented and atomized. These images of "immaculately happy families" are seen to support a form of "romantic social fantasy": this "warm, exclusive, perfected family" belies the contemporary reality of more complex family structures and networks and erases the other institutional settings in which people live their lives. However, the critical analysis of family photographs can allow us to read "against the grain," inviting the telling of hitherto suppressed stories and linking personal memory to broader public myths and political narratives. In the photographic work of Jo Spence (1986), this critique informs a kind of "counter-photography" that seeks to disrupt and deconstruct such conventional images, for example, by representing taboo or previously excluded aspects of family life, by problematizing the relation between photographer and subject, or by directly challenging or subverting traditional stereotypes.

In the case of Spence and her colleagues, this led to the development of a form of feminist "photo-therapy," which can involve participants reenacting images or scenes from their own family history in order to bring out and confront previously hidden contradictions and tensions (see Martin 1991; Spence 1991). Likewise, Annette Kuhn (1995) uses her own family photographs as the basis for a form of "memory work" that seeks to connect personal memory with collective or cultural memory. Delving behind photographs from her childhood, she reveals some of the hidden hostility and repression of her early family life, while linking this with national memories expressed in both documentary photographs and fictional films. Such work often focuses on the experience of upward class mobility and the feelings of inadequacy that can accompany it. It also draws to some extent on the inspiration of Roland Barthes (1984), whose reflections on a photograph of his own mother as a child form the basis of a broader meditation on grief and remembrance. Here, Barthes argues against the notion that photographs are "mere" representations: on the contrary, he suggests, they have an "evidential force"—they provide a "certificate of presence" that may be particularly powerful in the case of amateur rather than professional photographs. Marianne Hirsch (1997) makes similar use of photographs in exploring cultural memories of the Holocaust, while Michelle Citron (1998) uses home movies in an avant-garde feminist memoir of her early family life, which notably blurs settled distinctions between fact and fiction. These latter approaches all move beyond ideological critique toward a form of therapeutic practice that seeks in various ways to address the psychic and emotional dimensions of such images, although, in line with some feminist autobiography (e.g., Steedman 1986), individual subjective experiences are understood here in their relationship to the broader social and historical context. (These approaches are discussed further in relation to our data in chapter 4.)

A very different account of photography is provided by Pierre Bourdieu and his colleagues (Bourdieu et al. 1990). Like Chalfen's (1987), Bourdieu's concern is with photography as a social practice: he directly opposes psychological explanations (e.g., about the "needs" photography is seen to address or the "satisfactions" it offers) in favor of a sociological analysis of how the uses of this medium are socially organized and distributed. As with Chalfen, this means identifying the rules and conventions that define what is deemed to be "photographable," or appropriate subject matter for a photograph, and the social contexts in which photographs are produced and displayed. Bourdieu argues that the "family function" of photography is crucial, particularly for lower social classes: photography is used to mark formal occasions, to "solemnize" and "immortalize" the high points of family life, and to reinforce the integration of the family—although there are some "deviants," such as dedicated members of camera clubs, who reject such "ordinary" functions and aspire to a different set of aesthetic norms. Meanwhile, in some instances—for example, in the case of professionally produced wedding photographs or studio portraits of children, as distinct from "snapshots"—the photograph also faces outward to the wider world, enabling the family to assert its social position and influence relative to others. It is notable in this context, Bourdieu suggests, that "the arrival of the domestic practice of photography coincides with a more precise differentiation between what belongs to the public and what to the private sphere" (Bourdieu et al. 1990, 29)

As is the case with Bourdieu's work more broadly, his account of photography displays a somewhat deterministic view of social class. *Photography* was originally published in French in 1965, and it describes a world in which the distinctions among "peasants," "petit bourgeoisie," and "haute bourgeoisie" seem starkly defined. Gender is almost entirely absent as a dimension of analysis, which seems quite paradoxical when compared with the work of Spence, Kuhn, and others. Furthermore, while Bourdieu does provide some interesting reflections on the role of the family album in sustaining "social memory" (30–31), the psychic dimensions of such practices are clearly marginalized here. Even so, his work does provide a more strongly sociological analysis that can complement, rather than contradict, the insights of the feminist work discussed above.

THE VIDEO REVOLUTION?

As we noted in our introduction, one of the recurring claims about amateur media production is the idea that it can permit a wider democratization of media. Successive generations of political and academic commentators have asserted that gaining access to the "means of production" would empower individuals to give voice to hitherto marginalized experiences, to address social and political issues, and to create alternatives to dominant forms of representation. Such claims about the potential for "empowering" ordinary people have also been a recurring feature of popular discourse about amateur film and video making, not least in consumer magazines and advice manuals (see Buckingham, Pini, and Willett 2007).

Yet, until fairly recently, there has been little evidence that any such radical democratization has transpired. As we have seen, Zimmerman (1995) argues that in respect of home movie production, this potential for radical change was systematically defused by the growing dominance of the home mode, "thereby amputating its more resistant, economic and political potential for critique" (x). Similarly, Laurie Ouellette (1995) argues that amateur video has failed, or more precisely has not been allowed, to live up to its radical potential. Looking at the debut in the United States of television shows such as *I Witness Video* and *America's Funniest Home Videos,* Ouellette argues that the selection of amateur video footage that gets shown remains firmly within the home mode. As she suggests, the actual practice falls radically short of the hype that surrounded the debut of these shows, which typically presented video as a revolutionary tool that would bring "power to the people." Contrary to such claims, she argues, "the people" are anything but free to create their own programming. On the other hand, as Moran (2002, 51) suggests, there is a danger here of implying that people are simply passive dupes of ideology—that if they had not been brainwashed by Kodak commercials and their ilk, the masses would be spontaneously volunteering as grassroots video activists.

Even so, such claims about the empowering potential of amateur media production have significantly resurfaced with the advent of the Internet. Henry Jenkins (2006) focuses particularly on the ways in which fans are now becoming active and productive participants in media culture. Jenkins's notion of "convergence culture" refers partly to the technological convergence between different media that has been made possible by digitization and to the new transmedia franchises that have emerged in its wake (his most sustained example of this is *The Matrix*). However, it also refers to the convergence between producers and consumers that has accompanied this. Jenkins argues that technological change has enabled consumers to actively seek out new information and to make connections across an ever-wider range of cultural material. In this changing environment, we are seeing the emergence of a new "participatory culture" in which consumers—and particularly fans—are becoming producers of media, by appropriating, annotating, and reworking mainstream media content. According to Jenkins, this new "DIY" (do-it-yourself) vernacular culture is a key source of innovation that is pushing mainstream media in new directions. It is also a networked culture, which is creating new forms of "collective intelligence" that are more attuned to the mobility and fluidity of contemporary life: media audiences are organizing themselves into democratic "knowledge communities," which allow them to exercise greater collective power in relation to media producers.

Jenkins's examples range from fans of the TV show *Survivor* circulating online "spoilers" about future developments in the series, to writers of *Harry Potter* fan fiction or creators of *Star Wars* fan movies, to "modding" and "machinima" using material from computer games, to the use of participatory media such as blogging in the 2004 U.S. presidential election campaign. Jenkins's primary focus is on the interactions between fans and mainstream commercial media culture, and in this respect, there is a clear continuity with his earlier work on media fandom (Jenkins 1992): the difference now is that fan culture has become significantly more visible, more productive, and perhaps more powerful. Jenkins argues that digital technology has overcome many of the obstacles that led to the marginalization of previous amateur filmmaking, partly because of the accessibility and quality of digital editing but also because of the ease with which such material can be distributed online. The fan productions he describes are no longer "home movies" but "public movies," both in the sense that they can be circulated to wider audiences and in that they rework popular mythologies and engage in a public dialogue with mainstream commercial cinema (Jenkins 2006, 143).

The crucial question here, however, is the extent to which any of this amounts to a form of "empowerment"—and, indeed, what that might mean. As Jenkins shows, the media industries are very keen to exploit the possibilities of these new participatory media in their efforts to extend and deepen consumers' emotional identifications with their brands. They may occasionally find the productive activity of fans disruptive, challenging, and hard to handle, and this can result in struggles, particularly over copyright. However, there is a distinct danger here of overestimating, and indeed merely celebrating, the power of media fans. Contemporary media often depend upon "activity" on the part of consumers, but that does not necessarily mean that consumers are more powerful: *activity* should not be confused with *agency* (Buckingham and Sefton-Green 2003). Furthermore, since such activities are commercially driven, there are likely to be significant inequalities in the extent to which people are able to participate in them—inequalities that, as Jenkins acknowledges, are not simply to do with access to equipment, but with cultural capital and expertise (see also Jenkins et al. 2006).

Jean Burgess (2007) draws critically on some of Jenkins's ideas in her research on online photo sharing and "digital storytelling." Unlike most of Jenkins's examples, however, these forms involve the original production of images rather than the reworking of existing media content. Burgess argues that there is a danger of elitism if cultural studies academics focus primarily on the more spectacular or "cool" manifestations of this DIY culture, such as machinima, fan films, or video "mashups": such an emphasis can validate quasi-artistic (or perhaps merely "arty") practices at the expense of more "ordinary," less obviously innovative ones. Digital storytelling, in which people create short autobiographical films or multimedia presentations, is one example of the more mainstream "vernacular creativity" that Burgess explores—although, as she makes clear, it is a workshop-based process that tends to occur in quite specific institutional settings (in the United Kingdom, for example, it has largely been pioneered by the BBC). Such digital stories tend not to display the irony or witty reflexivity of many fan productions: on the contrary, they are typically sincere, poignant, gently humorous—and even somewhat "uncool."

Even so, the political implications of these developments remain to be seen. On one level, it is undoubtedly the case that "Web 2.0" technologies have offered significant new opportunities for communication among already established radical groups (Clark 2007)—although one would have to acknowledge that they have also served this function for extreme right-wing groups and, indeed, for conspiracy theorists and lunatics of all kinds. The case that remains to be made here is whether such technologies are genuinely "empowering" for those who are not already engaged or involved and in what ways. The extent of active participation, for example, in user-generated sites, is vastly less than is often assumed: one recent study suggested that only 0.16 percent of visitors to YouTube from the United States actually contribute videos (and most of these, of course, are not amateur productions), while only 0.20 percent of users upload images to the photo-sharing site Flickr (Auchard 2007). It is likely that those who make most use of such facilities are also well provided with other such opportunities in other areas of their lives; and so these technologies might in fact serve to widen the gaps between participants and nonparticipants rather than to reduce them.

Other commentators have pointed to a rather less sanguine account of these developments. Jon Dovey (2000) locates the use of portable video within a wider analysis of "first person media," which ranges from the overtly subjective documentaries of Nick Broomfield and Michael Moore to reality TV, talk shows, video diaries, and "docu-soaps." Such material is, of course, relatively cheap to produce, and it is partly for this reason that it has become significantly more prevalent on broadcast television in the years since Dovey's book was written. Dovey argues that these new forms represent a "foregrounding of individual subjective experience at the expense of more general truth claims" (26), which is symptomatic of broader cultural and social changes. This focus on personal identity can be seen as suitable fodder for the reflexive "project of the self" that theorists such as Anthony Giddens (1991) regard as characteristic of late modernity: such practices promise a degree of personal control and authentic individuality in a world that is increasingly experienced as unstable and chaotic. On the other hand, this proliferation of first-person forms might equally be seen as evidence of a new form of self-regulation and surveillance—a means of producing new norms of socially acceptable individuality and selfhood.

It is perhaps only a short step from here to the all-encompassing gloom of authors such as Frederic Jameson (1991)—or indeed, to the more popular account of the "death of culture" proffered by Andrew Keen (2007). From this perspective, the ubiquity of video and its seemingly irresistible permeation into all areas of public and private life is typically seen as symptomatic of a wider retreat into the "society of the spectacle"—a world of superficial images with only a tenuous relationship to what we once used to call reality. Ultimately, such totalizing rhetoric is no more convincing—and rather less seductive—than the optimistic claims about democratization with which we began.

CONCLUSION

These academic accounts of amateur creativity seem to impose a considerable weight of political and cultural expectation on what remains, at least for most people, a relatively mundane, unremarkable, everyday practice. On one level, it seems fairly absurd to expect home movies to express ideological critiques of the nuclear family, to generate radical forms of artistic experimentation, to give voice to social and political concerns, or indeed to contribute to the overthrow of patriarchy or capitalism. The fact that such things apparently fail to occur should not necessarily be a cause for disappointment or rejection. Rather, we would argue that the analysis of home video making provides more nuanced insights into the complex dynamics of family life, the social construction and representation of identity, and the nature of contemporary forms of cultural literacy—as well as generating a more realistic assessment of the potential contribution of the media to social change. Instead of regarding the home mode as inherently lacking or inadequate, or indeed as automatically ideologically or artistically conservative, we need to pay closer attention to what it is and how it works.

CHAPTER 2

Exploring the Home Mode: Researching Video Practices

The longer we have it, the less we use it. . . . You have this initial excitement about a new gadget and you play with it and that wears off. But then with time you also realize what it's good for and what its limitations are and what it imposes on the situation. (Yaron)

Because the research project was so long . . . [the camcorder] had its natural life. (Loren)

I haven't got anything to show you, but it's just to prove that things do get in the way. . . . Like when family life takes a bad turn, and it shows that . . . situations are different. (Nicole)

There are various ways in which we might have chosen to investigate the phenomenon of home video production. As part of our larger project (described in the introduction), we ran an online survey that provided us with a broad view of amateur video practices taking place in the United Kingdom. We asked about the technology amateur video makers were using, their motivations for purchasing equipment and making videos, and the communities they were involved in. As part of the same project, we also identified and interviewed different groups of amateur video producers, ranging from citizen journalists to skateboarders to amateur pornographers (see Buckingham and Willett 2009). From our survey and the individual interviews, we were able to analyze the cultural contexts of these amateur video practices and explore more individual aspects related to identity, learning, and creativity. However, the respondents to our survey were largely "serious amateurs" with a well-established interest in the area, and our case studies were mostly one-off snapshots of similarly committed video makers. Furthermore, this material did not give us information about the longitudinal aspects of amateur camcorder use referred to in the opening quotations of this chapter: once people have purchased a video camera, how do they learn to make videos, and how does this practice develop (or fail to develop) over time? The study reported in this book, therefore, involved more longitudinal and in-depth fieldwork with a relatively small group of participants. It provides us with data that are more complex than one-off interviews or survey responses, and it allows us to focus more closely on questions about how people use video cameras, how they learn about video making, the significance of what they make, and how this fits into the everyday dynamics of the household.

There is a long tradition of sociological and anthropological research on family life, particularly in urban settings. Key points of reference here would include Sandra Wallman's (1984) classic study of eight London households and more recent work such as Ruth Finnegan's (1998) account of the residents of the English "new town" of Milton Keynes. More directly relevant here is the anthropological work of Daniel Miller and his colleagues on the role of consumption within families—at least some of which has also involved families in diverse London neighborhoods (e.g., Miller 1998, 2008). However, our own approach primarily seeks to build on earlier studies of the use of media in the home—and as such, our main points of reference are drawn from media and cultural studies. Here, the early work of David Morley (1986) and Ann Gray (1992) on domestic uses of television and video respectively has led to a series of other studies, including some work by David Buckingham and others focusing on the role of parents (e.g., Buckingham 1996; Buckingham and Scanlon 2003; Buckingham and Bragg 2004; see also Hoover et al. 2004). As we mentioned in chapter 1, there is also a related body of research on the "domestication" of information and communication technologies—an approach we apply and develop in chapter 3.

In common with all these studies, our approach is resolutely qualitative. We have not sought to undertake a representative social survey or to make generalizations about the uses of video among particular social groups. Rather, we have attempted to understand how a particular medium or technology is appropriated and how its use is located within the internal dynamics and routines of everyday domestic life. In chapters 4 and 5 in particular, our analysis also addresses more psychological concerns to do with emotion, subjectivity, and learning. These issues require qualitative methods, which enable us to explore processes and practices in depth and detail. We would describe our approach as broadly "interpretivist," in that we are interested in exploring how individuals understand and give meaning to their everyday activities (cf. Silverman 2004). Our analysis considers public discourses concerning themes such as family, technology, creativity, and learning, and we analyze how these discourses are rehearsed, negotiated, or rejected in the participants' accounts of their activities. Further, we are interested in the different identities of the participants and how these are reflected in the videos they make and in the ways they present themselves to us as researchers. In this sense, our analysis is similar to the constructivist approach described by Hoover et al. (2004). In all these ways, we hope to have captured something of the complex and contingent ways in which people integrate a piece of technology into their daily lives and the diverse functions that it can come to serve for them.

Something of this is apparent in the quotations from our participants with which we began. Throughout the following chapters, the inflated claims from advertisements and how-to books described in chapter 1 are variously repeated, dismissed, and scoffed at by the participants in our study. We examine what camcorders were "good for" as well as their "limitations," we discuss the "natural life" of the camcorder, and we analyze the things that "get in the way" of using it. As our final quotation above suggests, different situations within each household significantly impacted the uses and meanings associated with the camcorder. But first, in this chapter, we introduce our 12 households and follow this with a discussion of our methodological approach. Accessing videos of private family events, watching interactions among family members on videos, discussing practices that happen in the privacy of homes—these are all aspects of the study that at times have raised uncomfortable feelings of voyeurism and even surveillance. The final part of this chapter, therefore, contains a discussion of participants' feelings about being research participants, as well as our own reflections on this delicate process.

PARTICIPATING HOUSEHOLDS

All our participants lived in the vicinity of our research lab in central London. We chose this area partly for reasons of convenience: it meant that the households were close enough for us to be able to exchange videotapes, deal with technical issues, and conduct interviews in homes with ease. However, it also made it possible for us to assemble a socioeconomically and ethnically mixed group of participants. We are based near Kings Cross, an inner city area with a striking mixture of characteristics. Once a major site of prostitution and drug use, the area is now (in the words of one local council's publicity materials) the site of "one of the largest and most complex programmes of planning and development-led regeneration in Europe" (Islington Council n.d.). The area is home to the new St. Pancras International station (with high-speed trains to Europe), and the redevelopment of its warehouses and brown-field land will include concert halls, shopping centers, restaurants, offices, and residential areas. As such, there are striking juxtapositions of wealth and poverty, deprivation and conspicuous consumption, and some significant social problems, particularly for young people.

The majority of households were recruited from a primary school in the area. In the United Kingdom, nearly half of parents with young children own camcorders, and we therefore felt that families from a primary school would be somewhat representative of domestic camcorder users (Mintel 2008). As a way of broadening the sample, participants were also recruited from a local community center. Flyers were distributed offering a free camcorder, detailing the project, and explaining the terms of participation, which involved taking part in three interviews over the course of 15 months and sharing a selection of videotapes. In the end we had only 14 applicants and chose 12 households that were considered more typical of everyday camcorder users (thus, e.g., declining to offer a camcorder to a couple who were professional filmmakers).

We did not intend to obtain a representative sample with such a small number, and in some ways the sample is untypical of UK households:

there are more participants with young children, more university graduates, and greater ethnic diversity than in the general population. The sample was diverse in many ways, not only in terms of ethnicity. There was a variety of ages and family structures. Some households were unambiguously professional middle-class, while in others we could see clear social-class "trajectories," with partners, grandparents, parents, and children moving across socioeconomic groups. While in some households, the parent(s) held university degrees, others were living in government-supported housing and working in unskilled or semiskilled jobs. Eight of the households included two parents living with their child or children, three were single mothers living with their child or children, and one consisted of a single retired man. One household was black (African Caribbean), one was Asian (Bangladeshi), and one was mixed Asian and white. The other nine were all white, although of very diverse nationalities, including British, Australian, German, Israeli, Irish, and one from the former Soviet republic of Georgia. All except one household lived in rented and/or government-supported accommodation.

We were interested in seeing if participants would edit their videos or post them on the Internet (given the rhetoric discussed in chapter 1). We therefore ensured that all households had a computer that was at most four years old or at least had access to a computer. Once recruited, participants were invited to the university, where we spoke with them individually about the project and what was expected from them, and they were given brief general instructions on how to use the camcorder (they also had the instruction manual). A basic entry-level domestic camcorder was given to each household, along with 10 DV tapes and a diary for recording the date and content of each video session. In addition to conducting interviews, we asked the participants to select tapes for us to view, which we copied to disk and then returned. The households kept the camcorders at the end of the project.

Below are details of the 12 households, with the names in subheadings (at the start of each description) of the video makers who are mainly referred to in the following chapters. The ages of the children given here are those at the start of the project. All names are pseudonyms. We are aware that it will be difficult for readers to keep all these details in mind as they read on, and we have therefore provided a brief "hook line" for each one in order to help with this. It is difficult to summarize complex family dynamics over 15 months, and we apologize to the participants for simplifying them at this point. However, the following chapters will build on these snapshots and present what we hope is a more complex and rounded picture.

Aidan and Ted (age 10)—Sharks, School Discos, and Spoofs

Aidan and Sarah, who are both white British, live in a rented apartment with their three children: Zac (11), Ted (10), and Issy (3). Sarah is an art teacher, and Aidan is a freelance writer and designer. Both have degree-equivalent qualifications. Aidan and Sarah had previously considered purchasing a camcorder for their son Ted, who had been using the video function on Sarah's still camera to make short scripted films. When the camcorder we gave them was damaged (as a result of trying to get some underwater shots for Ted's sequel to *Jaws*), they invested in a new one, in spite of the financial difficulties this caused. This family was therefore already emotionally (and then financially) invested in using a camcorder.

Initially Aidan aimed to use the camcorder for "family events, play and experimentation," and during interviews he discussed developing a video album for each child. The family produced a variety of footage of family get-togethers and children's performances, homemade "spoofs," and dramatic play. The camcorder was shared primarily between Aidan and his sons, with Sarah continuing to capture images on her still camera. The camcorder was always out of its case in this household, with a second battery plugged in for recharging, and Ted in particular provided us with various bits of playful footage (lip-synching to pop songs and playing pretend soccer matches with his sister). Ted also orchestrated various sketches (based on *Jaws, Lost, Doctor Who,* and a Nike advertisement) that involved considerable amounts of planning, preparation, and family participation.

Bruno and Klaus (age 7)—Vacations and Performances

Bruno lives with his wife, Heike, and their 7-year-old son, Klaus. They used to live in Kings Cross but have since bought their own Victorian terraced house in a gentrifying area of inner London. The house is elegantly furnished and extremely tidy. The family is white, originally from Germany, and recently settled in the United Kingdom. Bruno is a university lecturer, and Heike is a foreign media correspondent. Both Bruno and Heike have completed Ph.D.s.

Bruno was interested in obtaining a camcorder for a number of reasons, including learning (with Klaus) about editing, lighting, and video making generally; videotaping what he called "various physics contraptions" (such as marble and domino runs); and possibly as part of his job as a lecturer. It was mainly Bruno and Klaus who produced footage, which included holidays abroad and various family gatherings and school performances. Klaus also worked on a video tour of their newly acquired house and did a few performance-related projects with Bruno (a magic trick and piano skit). Near the end of the project, Klaus learned editing at school and started to work with Bruno on producing some edited footage.

Edward—Scenes from a London Bus

Edward (age 70), a white, retired London bus driver and inspector, lives alone in a rented apartment. Edward is a keen photographer (with a qualification in the subject), and the walls of his apartment are covered with professional-looking photographs he has taken. He is closest, of all the participants, to what we might call a "serious amateur" (Stebbins 2007), though he resisted joining a film and video making club. This was partly because of previous unpleasant experiences with such organizations, but also because he sees himself as "more than just a hobbyist" (by which he means someone who does not want to go further than a hobby). Edward says he would "love" to do video and photography professionally and is a member of a photography club.

Edward was the most prolific video maker among our participants, using 12 tapes and asking for more. The bulk of his footage consists of London scenes taken from buses, trains, a river boat, and on foot. However, he also videotaped his daughter's family Christmas, a Christmas party at his pensioners' club, and the opening of the recently renovated St. Pancras station. (The latter two videos were screened within his photography and pensioners' clubs.) He indicated that he would like to make videos for people who (either through disability or because they live overseas) cannot travel around London. Edward was the only participant with no immediate access to a computer (although we were told he could have access at the community center). However, he claimed that he felt no need to edit his videos and included credits by videotaping envelopes with his name and address on at the start of each tape.

Jocelyn—from Script Writing to "Video Postcards"

Jocelyn, originally from Australia, lives with her 6-year-old son, Jack, in their rented apartment. Both are white. Jocelyn has a bachelor of arts degree and works as an administrator in a publishing house. Jocelyn has a keen interest in editing, which is connected with her previous employment working with film editors. She wants to develop her production skills, possibly as a way into further jobs within creative industries, and at the beginning of the project, she aimed to script, videotape, and edit short productions. By the end, however, she said she was focusing on scriptwriting as her creative outlet and using the camcorder more as a means to develop a family archive.

Jocelyn was interested in taking part in the project because her son liked taking photographs, and she imagined that owning a camcorder would provide an opportunity for them to make a video together. Jocelyn's video footage covers everyday interactions with Jack (reading, eating, playing games, doing crafts), as well as footage from various special events and vacations. Jack occasionally used the camcorder when Jocelyn had it out. With parents in Hong Kong and brothers in Australia, Jocelyn aimed to edit her footage and e-mail "video postcards" to share with her family special events and short "day-in-the-life" videos of their life in London. After receiving home videos from family abroad, Jocelyn was keen to eliminate repetitive or boring sequences from the videos she sent in return and was one of the few participants who edited some of their footage.

Leslie and Matt—Sharing with Grandma

Leslie and Matt live with their daughters, Rachel (5) and Anne (3), in rented accommodations. Leslie is an early-years educator, currently undertaking a part-time degree in teaching, and Matt is a factory worker. Leslie is white (Irish), and Matt is white (English). Leslie's main reason for wanting to take part in the project was to videotape her children dancing and singing and to send the footage to her mother.

Much of Leslie and Matt's footage is of their daughters performing, playing, or doing everyday activities around their home or on family or school outings. Throughout our discussions, Matt (who has a small music studio and is familiar with synthesizer technology) was constructed as the technologically interested one, while Leslie was slower to adapt to the camcorder and used it mainly to videotape school performances. In addition to collecting footage, Matt transferred all the videos to DVDs (for storage) and also created very roughly edited VHS tapes for his mother (who lives in southern England) and for Leslie's family in Ireland. Matt described himself as being quite spontaneous and relaxed with the camcorder, whereas Leslie had to be "in the right frame of mind" and often found the whole practice "a bit of a grief." As time went on, however, Leslie said that she had become more relaxed, less self-conscious, and more confident about using the camcorder. The daughters were keen to be videotaped, reminding Leslie to bring the camcorder to school for their performances, and near the end of the project Rachel received her own still camera with a video function, which she used to make films of her dolls.

In some senses, Leslie and Matt represent one of our more "successful" cases of camcorder usage. Leslie became more confident, the camcorder was integrated into their family life, and they achieved their aim of sharing footage with the girls' grandmothers. As discussed in chapter 3, this was partly because of their moderate aspirations at the start of the project but also because of Matt's skills and position as both a father and a son.

Loren and Barney (age 13) — Memories of Family Life

Loren lives with her two sons, 13-year-old Barney and 11-year-old Joe, in rented public housing. All are white, with Loren originally coming from Australia. Loren has a bachelor of arts degree in visual arts and is a jewelry designer and director of her own jewelry design company. Loren's footage is very much family-based, centering on her sons, and videos are made with her Australian parents' viewing in mind. Loren saw the video as a means of preserving memories, and when she forgot to pack the camcorder on a major family vacation to Australia, she said she was heartbroken.

Loren initially anticipated that she would use the camcorder to video her sons' activities, as well as special family occasions, in order to send videos to her parents. She did manage this to some extent, while Barney became quite active in producing his own footage, including videos of general play and "larking around," sports, and social gatherings. Barney was also involved in the grime music scene in his peer group, and he aimed to videotape his friend's rap crew and upload it on MySpace, though this never happened. Joe also used the camcorder on occasion, though he felt awkward and did not develop an interest in videotaping as the project progressed. Barney and Joe also took the camcorder when they went away with their father, videotaping activities such as skiing for Loren and other family members to view. As far as we know, Loren was the only participant who produced what we might call a video diary, which was her narration about the process of being rehoused by the local council.

Mariya and Mikhael—Georgians in London

Mariya and Mikhael lived with their daughter, 7-year-old Alisa, in university housing. The family is white and was visiting from the former Soviet republic of Georgia. At the start of the project, Mariya was undertaking a master's degree course in educational policy, and Mikhael was working in the field of educational technology. Just before the end of the project, the family returned to their home in Georgia. Mariya and Mikhael had friends and relatives in various countries, including Poland, Russia, Estonia, and Georgia, with whom they aimed to share videos. Although this did not happen due to time and technical constraints, Mikhael did manage to e-mail a few videos he had made on his camera phone.

Mariya imagined many uses for the camcorder and spoke about wanting to participate in citizen journalism, join groups online, make animations with Alisa, and share videos of the United Kingdom with policy makers in Georgia as a way of effecting change (e.g., in educational practice). However, much of the video footage we viewed was of family and friends and scenes around London. Mariya described herself as a "CCTV kind of filmer," taking the camera everywhere and focusing on details, whereas she described Mikhael as more selective, less dynamic, and more traditional. At the start of the project, Mikhael used the camcorder to record special family get-togethers and scenes from Georgia, but by the end he saw more value in videotaping for future memories and said he was surprised at the pleasure he gained from capturing everyday interactions.

Neil—Inner City Pressure

Neil, a black British 17-year-old, lives with his mother, 11-year-old brother, and 14-year-old sister. In addition to studying for his school exams, Neil had many demands on his time—he frequently had several choices of activities in the evenings, including drama, football, drug awareness activities, a youth forum, and dances. In the second year of the project, Neil started studying business and law at a local university. Although he was still living at home, we lost contact with Neil and were not able to complete the final interview.

Neil originally indicated that he wanted to be part of the project because of his enjoyment of film but also because he was interested in making videos that would "give an insight into life in WC1" (the project's postal code). He was involved in the local grime music scene and spoke about making videos to upload on MySpace as well as more documentary-style videos of the different grime groups. This never came about, partly because of conflicts among the different groups of young people in the area, known as "postcode gangs." Both Neil and his brother used the camcorder to produce a variety of footage. This included video of a local football match, birthday celebrations in the home, tours of the apartment, and general "larking about" (including rapping). Neil's sister also used the camcorder, though we were not able to view any of her footage. Neil also spoke at length about videotaping "conflicts" between his mother and sister, which he showed to them afterward (and kept private from us). This practice operated partly as a way for Neil to remove himself from the scene, but he also hoped that the videos would help his sister to "look back on her actions later on" and rethink her behavior.

Nicole, Felix (age 14), and Lexi (age 10)—Life Getting in the Way

Nicole lives with her husband, Peter, and their two children, 14-year-old

Felix and 10-year-old Lexi, in their rented family home. Nicole is an ICT (Information, Communication, and Technology) tutor and learning mentor in schools and has a national vocational qualification. Peter describes himself as having no qualifications and works as an operations manager for a fruit and vegetable supplier. Both are white British. On the application, Nicole wrote that having a camcorder would enable her to record family outings and special events. She also hoped to learn about basic editing.

The main camcorder users were Nicole, Felix, and occasionally Lexi. Peter, who is described by Nicole as "not very technical," rarely used the camcorder. During the first six months of the project, they filmed family outings, special occasions, and school-related events. Nicole had many ideas about what she wanted to do with the camcorder, including a video styled after the TV show *Property Ladder,* which would chart the progress of the family's work on their recently acquired house. By our third interview, Nicole and Peter were facing what she described as a big family "trauma" that had left them with serious financial problems, and as a result, Nicole had taken on extra employment. Problems around time and money (fewer outings and holidays), as well as changes in the children's activities (fewer competitions and public performances), meant that very little video was actually produced during this final stage.

Phil—Comedy Skits and Family Life

At the start of the study, Phil and Ruba lived with their three children (two sons, age 15 years and 7 months, and one daughter, age 4) in rented public housing. Fourteen months into the project, the family moved out of London to be close to the school where their older son was enrolled. Phil is white British, and Ruba is British Asian. Phil is a freelance folk musician, and Ruba is a clinical psychologist. Phil indicated that they were interested in owning a camcorder for two main reasons: to film their family and possibly to use in the production of a promotional video for his music.

Phil was almost always the one who videotaped, and he had a range of ideas about what to make, including music videos to put on MySpace and comedy skits, as well as videos of everyday family life, outings, and get-togethers. Phil and Ruba have family living abroad and in other parts of

England, and they imagined sending videos to share with them. In addition to the variety of material that Phil videotaped, he often experimented with things such as camera angles (lying down with the camcorder on his chest while the children climbed on him or simply leaving the camcorder running on the kitchen counter during a meal). Phil tended to classify his video making as mainly family based, though he was critical of what he saw as the "normal" use of family photography and video, seeing his own family videos as more mundane, "natural," and spontaneous.

Shanta—Children's Performances and Family Gatherings

Shanta lives with her husband, Mahaz, and their children (a 7-year-old son and a 10-year-old daughter) in rented housing. Shanta and her husband both come from Bangladesh, where they still have relatives. Shanta is a classroom assistant at the school that her children attend. This family had some unfortunate experiences related to the project: the camcorder was stolen with a recording of the family trip to Bangladesh for Shanta's father's funeral (we subsequently replaced it), one of the videotapes was lost in the mail, and Shanta was not able to download footage to her computer.

The bulk of Shanta's footage is heavily family based, including special occasions (Eid), children's performances (school plays, recitations of the Quran), and family gatherings. Shanta comes from a large, close-knit Bangladeshi family that views footage of children's performances at family gatherings and passes it around to members of the extended family who cannot attend. Mahaz rarely used the camcorder because, in Shanta's terms, he could not see the point in amassing lots of family footage. However, he did use it quite extensively when visiting Bangladesh to videotape scenery he remembered from his childhood.

Yaron—The Limitations of Technology

Yaron and his wife, Hinda, both white, live with their 10-year-old son and their 6-year-old daughter in rented university housing. Yaron is currently employed as a university researcher in the field of education and technology, and Hinda is an architect. Both have higher degrees and come from Israel.

The family produced a variety of footage, including the children at home, school performances and sports activities, and visits to Israel with friends and family. Footage was produced primarily by Yaron and his son, although Hinda and the 6-year-old daughter took the camcorder on occasion. Yaron is one of the few participants who edited and shared footage with friends and family online. By the end of the project, he commented that the initial excitement of having the camcorder had worn off, and they were using it less often. He said he was aware of collecting hours of footage that would never get watched and so was trying to record less during each videotaping session—particularly as he felt he would need to edit it in order to make it "watchable." He said the experience made him more aware of limitations of the technology—both of the difficulty and inconvenience of using it and of the intrusion the camcorder can create.

TALKING ABOUT VIDEO MAKING PRACTICES

We conducted three semistructured interviews with each participating household over the course of 15 months, going into homes when possible and otherwise interviewing at the university. Two of us were present at each interview, all of which were recorded and then transcribed. Interview questions included general inquiries about what participants had been doing in terms of videotaping, sharing, and editing (where applicable), with specific inquiries related to our broad research themes and questions.

We were keen to assure the participants that we were not expecting anything in particular from their camcorder use: we were not looking for spectacular expressions of creativity and were just as interested in their seemingly mundane uses—and indeed, nonuses—of the equipment. We also wanted to reduce, if possible, their feelings of being "researched," a position enforced by their obligation to us as recipients of the camcorders and our positions as (middle-class, white) academics. To establish a more equal power dynamic, we tried to meet with participants in their homes. This also gave us some revealing information on their backgrounds, as expressed in the kinds of objects in their households (pictures, books, newspapers, technology), as well as enabling us to view and discuss video files they had on their computers. During the first and second interviews, we asked very open-ended questions about what they had been doing with the camcorders and whether or not they had used the manuals, shared videos with anyone, transferred videos, and so on. These interviews were informal and conversational, and we tried to relate our own experiences of home video making to their comments. For the third interview, we sent more formal questions beforehand, to give the participants a chance to reflect on their 15 months of use and allow us to raise more general issues.

The themes that emerged from the data (the interviews and the videos) cover a range of issues, which are addressed in the following chapters. While there are bound to be overlaps and connections, the topics addressed in each chapter are reasonably distinct. In focusing on these themes, there is an inevitable risk that we lose a sense of each individual household or participant. However, we believe this cross-cutting approach is more engaging (and ultimately less tedious to read) than a blow-by-blow account of each specific case study. By allowing us to compare the different households, it enables us to develop more general arguments and to connect the findings of our study to broader themes in social and cultural research. Even so, it is not easy to paint a picture that gives readers enough information to follow each of the participants, much less to portray them as we feel we know them. We therefore hope that readers will refer back to the brief descriptions in this chapter as they read further.

METHODOLOGICAL DILEMMAS

Although we were trying to approximate the situation of households receiving a camcorder for the first time (as a gift or as their own purchase), this was clearly not the case. Because the participants did not have to invest their own resources in purchasing the camcorder, they did not have to make decisions about how much they needed or wanted it or who it was for. The camcorders were gifts, in a way, but they came with strings attached. Participants signed contracts promising to take part in interviews and share some videos. Although we assured participants that we had no expectations, that it was perfectly acceptable and interesting if the camcorder never made it out of its box, they all indicated that they were aware of themselves being research participants (or subjects).

In most cases this awareness led participants to feel a need to produce more video (or more interesting video) than perhaps they might otherwise have done—or at least a feeling of guilt when they failed to do so. Only Phil suggested that he felt *less* obligated to use the camcorder as a research participant than if he had actually purchased the camcorder himself: as he said, "I would start to think I ought to use the thing if I've paid for it." Several participants apologized when we contacted them for the interviews, suggesting we interview them at a later time, after they had more opportunity to use the camcorder (e.g., after a summer vacation). During the interviews, individuals said they were "embarrassed," felt "awful," or felt they were leading us on a "wild goose chase" because they had little or no video data to share. At the end of the project, when we asked if their use would change knowing that they would no longer be meeting with us, most admitted to feeling an obligation to produce video throughout the project—though in fact they did not think that they actually had produced more than they would have done anyway. Two participants who were involved in academic research as part of their careers admitted to feeling obligated to produce "data" that we would regard as creative or interesting. Yaron explained:

> I feel like there is an implicit contract. . . . And you feel like, OK, we agreed to participate in this research so we have to kind of show some interesting, we have to generate interesting data and you're not [doing it], you know? [laughs] I mean, I know it's ridiculous, but it's there.

Although these feelings of guilt may not have led to more use or different kinds of uses, in some cases we did see evidence that the participants' activities were influenced by the research process. Yaron told us that the only time his children took the initiative in using the camcorder on their own was after we had interviewed the family, and Edward clearly stated that he made the videos for us to watch, expressing serious disappointment when we could not view all of his video data. (Edward requested detailed feedback from us about the content [possibly regarding skill and style] of all his videos and told us several times of another "university professor" who had viewed and appreciated the content of his photographs.) Other participants mentioned that they were aware that someone was going to watch their videos—although the tapes they passed on to us were entirely of their own choosing. Leslie said that she did not want to videotape without first tidying the house; and Mariya suggested that, possibly due to her Soviet background, she was always aware of being judged and wanting to be a "good subject." Certainly, some participants seemed keen to present themselves as "good research subjects." Jocelyn, for instance, said, with slight irony, "It's inspiring me to make films, there you go. That's what the camcorder has done to my life, how it's changed me." Mariya also sent us an extended thank you note, saying:

> I have learned new things about myself and my family, our tastes, our views and that is very valuable as an experience. You have contributed greatly to some wonderful events in our life and thank you for that. Many thanks on behalf of our daughter, Alisa, who will be enjoying her childhood videos in her adult life.

One further aspect of the research process that several participants mentioned was being given 10 free tapes. Only Edward used all his tapes, but several participants said they were aware that they did not have to videotape selectively in order to conserve tapes, as they might well have done otherwise. As a result, they did not have to make choices about what footage to keep or record over, or invest time and energy in transferring the footage in order to free up tapes.

The awareness of being watched borders on surveillance; and we were aware that our position as middle-class white academics was a factor in how participants felt during the interviews (Reay 1996; Walkerdine 1986). This was particularly true with Neil. In one interview, he described feeling that he was constantly under surveillance as a young black man, telling us about how CCTV cameras would "follow" him when he was in shops. This conversation made us more aware of our own surveillance of Neil and how this was reflected in our relationship with him: we had difficulties contacting him (he regularly failed to show up for interviews, we repeatedly had unanswered phone messages and letters, and we completely lost touch with him toward the end of the project). We were also unable to visit his home or meet his siblings, and he was reluctant to share any video data with us.

One final methodological issue we faced was in viewing and analyzing the videos. Aside from the uneasy feelings of surveillance and voyeurism, watching the videos was hard work. This material clearly meant far more to the participants than it did to us; and what we make of it depends very much on what our participants chose to tell us about it. As we discuss in the following chapters, participants saw such material as holding many possibilities for future use: they were convinced that someday they would review, edit, and share all their tapes. For most, however, this was only likely to occur at some unspecified time in the future: in fact, we found that many had not even watched their own videos more than once.

Furthermore, we were only able to view selections of the videos made by each participant, and in many cases, the participants referred to things they or their children had done or were planning to do that we were unable to verify in the videos themselves. In several cases, there was also a gap between what participants said and what we saw in the video data. There are several possible reasons for this. Participants might have felt pressure to perform for us during the interviews, to be "good research subjects," or to live up to the marketing hype about domestic camcorder use; we might not have been given videos with particular footage that was discussed in the interviews; or participants' interpretation of a piece of footage might have been different from ours. In most cases we watched some footage with the participants, but we had on average 6 hours of footage from each household, and we clearly could not watch all the footage together.

CONCLUSION

The research we report in this book is clearly only one possible way in which we might have investigated home video making. Although we did watch a great many of our participants' productions, we were not able to spend much time observing them. As such, we are reliant to a great extent on the stories they chose to tell us and hence on how they might have wished to present themselves, although we have tried to cross-check our data in a systematic way and to avoid simply taking what participants said at face value. Our research also involved a form of experimental intervention: giving the households a camcorder and then tracking what they did with it inevitably changed what they might have done otherwise—although again, we hope we have been sufficiently reflexive about this process here.

As with all qualitative research, there is a danger that we lose sight of the bigger picture, and in future work, we would hope to locate individuals' media making practices within a wider social and economic context. Even so, we would argue that a study of this nature potentially has a great deal to contribute to our broader understanding, for example, of contemporary changes in family life, or of the role of media and consumer culture, or even of the diversity of modern urban life. We can certainly speculate about these issues; but for the moment, our aim is simply to analyze some of the ways in which video making is carried out in everyday domestic setting and to explore some of the functions that it serves.

CHAPTER 3

Domesticating Video

> The household is a space where technology is adopted, consumed, argued about and, with varying degrees of success, integrated into domestic culture: the site where technology as an object and as mediator of public culture is shaped to meet the needs and reproduce the values of the home. (Ward 2006, 150)

This chapter focuses on where and when camcorders were used in our 12 households and for what purposes. On the surface, these aspects of camcorder use appear quite basic and obvious. However, as indicated in the opening quotation, the starting point for this chapter is an understanding of the camcorder as a site of negotiated meanings, where public discourses and practices enter the private space of the home. In this respect, the chapter builds upon previous work about the "domestication" of technology briefly introduced in chapter 1 (e.g., Silverstone and Hirsch 1992; Haddon 2004; Berker et al. 2006). It explores how the meanings of technology are shaped in the household, at the level of both discourse and everyday practice.

As we have noted, the domestication-of-technology approach can partly be seen as a reaction to technological determinism—that is, the view of technology as having "effects" (e.g., on family life), irrespective of how it is used. In terms of media studies, it represents a shift away from a focus on "texts and readers" to an analysis of the social contexts in which media are used, although, in common with that earlier research, it continues to regard consumers as active "meaning makers" (see Morley 1992). There have been numerous empirical studies within this tradition exploring the everyday uses of technologies and the social and cultural contexts in which they are located, although, as we have pointed out, these have effectively neglected the use of media *production* technologies such as film, photography, and video.

As we discussed in chapter 1, the use of camcorders in the home is often framed by celebratory claims about their ease of use, their potential to "unleash creativity" in users, and their role in capturing and displaying the "magic moments" of family life. These discourses are particularly prevalent in advertisements and consumer advice literature, and it is this material that typically informs people's decisions to purchase a camcorder in the first place. In relation to the 12 households in this study, although the camcorders were given to them (and therefore they did not make a decision to buy them), their ambitions both at the outset and throughout the project reflected these widespread celebratory claims. Ideas about the power of technology, then, accompanied the physical object of the camcorder as it was incorporated (or not) into the households.

However, the camcorder was also framed by a set of existing structures, relationships, and values characteristic of the specific households. Within each household, this was reflected in a range of practices, including the physical placement of the camcorder (safely tucked away high on a cupboard shelf or out in the open for anyone to access), how it was used, who used it, and when it was used, as well as how the camcorder itself and the subsequent footage were displayed and used outside the home. These practices were informed in turn by particular dynamics within each household. Thus, the camcorder could be seen as a piece of technology for use only by the technologically competent members of the family, as an everyday object alongside other technologies in the household, or as a facilitator for special creative and educational projects.

Previous research on the domestication of technology has addressed several of these issues. The broad aim of this research is to examine both the "macro" structures that are present in households and in discourses surrounding technology and the "micro" structures operating as the technology gets used and goes on display. This work has analyzed the interplay and intersection between the public and the private spaces in which technologies are situated, looking at the dynamics of power within households and the different phases or moments of domestication. This approach recognizes that households are sites of consumption, as well as sites with specific skills, cultural and aesthetic values, and social connections—all of which, when combined, constitute what is termed the "moral economy" of the household (Silverstone et al. 1992).

Thus, in our research, camcorders were used differently across the households and took on various meanings dependent on the experiences, histories, and values within each of them. Having a history of collecting keepsakes, valuing the recording of children's achievements, placing importance on family celebrations, having particular family members who were considered the technology experts—all of these were part of the moral economy of the households that impacted the uses and meanings of the camcorder.

Earlier studies have analyzed how technologies (e.g., television, computers, and mobile phones), which are potentially part of the everyday life of a household, go through different phases as they are introduced into a home—although the phases overlap, are not necessarily linear, and sometimes do not happen (Silverstone and Hirsch 1992; Berker et al. 2006). This starts with *commodification* (which also involves *appropriation*), as the technology is "sold" to the consumer. As Roger Silverstone describes, "Machines and services do not come into the household naked. They are packaged, certainly, but they are also 'packaged' by the erstwhile purchaser and user, with dreams and fantasies, hopes and anxieties: the imaginaries of modern consumer society" (2006, 234). The commodification/appropriation stage is thus invested with social meanings, as well as the functional action of obtaining the technology. Who decides to purchase the item, how the item is viewed as fitting into the household and for what purposes, and the rhetoric surrounding the item (as described in chapter 1 in relation to camcorders) are all part of this phase. For some people, the consumer item remains at this phase—items are purchased (or purchased on behalf of someone), and the technology remains as a container of *imagined* uses. (The classic line "I'll use it more when I have a bit of time" was one we repeatedly heard from the busy parents in our study.) As we shall see, in relation to some aspects of video making such as editing or organizing video footage, we saw this phase lasting throughout the 15 months of participation. With complex new technologies in particular, and with continuing inflated hype concerning their power and capacity, this phase is in some ways bound to exist alongside other phases.

The next two phases, *objectification* and *incorporation,* have been the focus of much of the research on the domestication of technologies. Objectification concerns how the object is physically placed in the household and how this placement reflects the values and relationships within it. Incorporation then concerns how the technology comes to function in the daily life of the household. People's perceptions of technology are particularly important in the incorporation stage. When a technology is defined as something unconnected with one's identity or outside one's usual purposes, incorporation is less likely to happen. Furthermore, family relations and power dynamics impact on incorporation of technology, particularly in relation to gender and age (Gray 1992).

Increasingly, networks outside the home are part of the incorporation of technologies within the home. Various technologies, including camcorders, are used for connecting with absent family members or new globalized networks. Importantly, these connections can provide audiences for people's work, community support, and motivation for further learning. Friends and relatives who are able to help novices with technology—"warm experts" in Leslie Haddon's (2004) terms—are particularly important during the incorporation stage. Warm experts not only give technical advice but also guide how technologies can be used.

The *conversion* phase, which has been less frequently analyzed in this body of research, is when the object becomes taken for granted, and its use or value is projected into the wider society in some manner. With an increase in mobile and productive technologies, such as the camcorder or camera phone, and with more households generating media content and sharing it online, this phase is perhaps growing in importance. Like other research in this area, our study has limited evidence of this phase, possibly due to various kinds of barriers to use, which we analyze in this chapter and in chapter 5.

Across all the phases of domestication, the objects themselves are invested with particular meanings as material consumer items: for example, camcorders may be seen as playthings, family record keepers, or important communication tools. However, there are also meanings attached with and negotiated through the objects: watching a video might elicit nostalgic views of a particular family vacation, for example. The analysis over the next three chapters therefore considers how the camcorder and the video footage it generates were integrated into the households and the meanings that were created in the process. In Silverstone, Hirsch, and Morley's terms, the analysis recognizes the "double articulation" of technology in households—"the ways in which information and communication technologies, uniquely, are the means (the media) whereby public and private meanings are mutually negotiated; as well as being the products themselves, through consumption, of such negotiations of meaning" (1992, 28).

INTERPRETING THE HOME MODE

As discussed in chapter 1, previous analyses have focused on the functional properties of amateur film and video making at a fairly general level (Zimmerman 1995; Moran 2002). The major exception to this is Richard Chalfen's (1987) *Snapshot Versions of Life,* which includes an extensive analysis of domestic video productions themselves, or what he terms "home mode" material. Camcorder technology has developed significantly since Chalfen's study: falling costs of camcorders have increased accessibility, and the switch to digital formats potentially makes editing easier, while the development of online video sharing sites has created new opportunities for video distribution. However, Chalfen's analysis of the key characteristics of home mode material applies very easily to the videos collected in our study. Chalfen analyzed the participants, topics, settings, and codes in home movies and family photographs, looking at what was present as well as what was absent. According to Chalfen, "we find a *special* reality documented in the home movie. Commonplace behaviour, mundane activities, and everyday happenings do *not* get recorded" (1987, 69, original emphasis). Similarly, in our study, although we saw videos of everyday occurrences such as the preparation of meals, eating, and children playing, we only saw particular aspects of day-to-day household activities.

In terms of *participants* in videos, in both Chalfen's study and ours, the main participants were people, especially children, relatives, and close friends. Videos focusing primarily on other subjects such as landscapes, wildlife, and household objects were rare. Further, people who might have been encountered on a regular basis in daily life, such as teachers or shopkeepers, did not feature in our videos, and the people shown were generally awake, alive, and well. Videotaping sleeping people occurred only as part of an idealized image ("sleeping like a baby") or as a joke (grandfather asleep at the family dinner table).

Chalfen argues that the *topics* of video show a "small fraction of everyday-life-at-home . . . combined with a lot of unusual-life-away-from-home" (1987, 61). As in Chalfen's study, many of our videos focused on vacations, holiday celebrations, local activities (such as playing in the garden), and special events. Although parts of everyday life were videotaped, these were particular selections of life: meals, but not the cleaning up after the meal; young children in the bathtub, but not on the toilet; the first day of school, but not other days. *Settings* were also selective—our home videos featured living and dining rooms, gardens, local parks, and more special places (school assembly halls, vacation sites, relatives' houses), but we rarely saw unsightly locations. Furthermore, videos were most frequently watched at home, in the living room or shared family space. Even with the advent of video sharing sites, the practice of viewing home videos has not moved to more public spaces (although camera phones may be changing this: see Willett 2009). Finally, the *codes* of home movies included lots of panning, zooming, and jump cuts; they were dominated by long and medium shots; and there was often little visual continuity (e.g., a video would jump from a birthday party to a vacation on a beach).

It is important to note that these points are not intended as critiques of home mode videos. One of Chalfen's aims in analyzing the characteristics of home movies is to contrast them with discussions in "how-to-do-it" manuals and to suggest that home movie makers and their audiences have different purposes for filming and viewing and different criteria for evaluating films. Thus, when we watch a home video, we are not necessarily concerned with continuity, and we forgive jump cuts. (However, as we shall see in chapter 5, most of our participants said that they found panning and zooming distracting when viewing, and they improved their videos by reducing these aspects.) The functions of home video are crucially different from the functions of other kinds of moving-image texts, and the people who make and watch them are generally well aware of this.

Chalfen identifies three functions of home mode productions: documentation, memory, and cultural membership. The *documentary* functions include creating a personal visual history, as well as validation of an experience, one's social self, and one's personal relationships. This is partly about the construction of the self, albeit "less perhaps of the idiosyncratic aspects of the individual, autonomous self, and more of the conforming, corporate-family self" (1987, 124). The *memory* function of videos is connected with capturing and reliving particular experiences and generally operates in nostalgic and hedonistic ways (enjoying the moment and repeating that pleasure through viewing). Finally, Chalfen's *cultural membership* category refers to the function of images that show people "conforming to social norms, achieving status and enjoying themselves, in part, as a result of a life well lived"; in short, the function is to display "a knowledge, capability, and competence to do things 'right'" (139). This last function connects with the conversion stage of the domestication of technology, the point at which the camcorder articulates the private values and practices of the household to a more public audience (family, friends, or even wider social contacts). Generally, the interviewees in our study discuss the functions of their video making in the terms outlined by Chalfen, although the functions clearly overlap, with any one piece of footage possibly serving all three functions.

Our analysis in this chapter includes a discussion of the components and functions of home video and extends Chalfen's account to include more performative and public types of video making practice. This chapter also analyzes the phases of domestication, particularly the commodification and incorporation stages, as well as addressing some barriers to incorporation. We begin with an analysis of the participants' aims in using the camcorder over the 15 months of the project, as well as their projected ambitions for future camcorder use. As discussed in chapter 2, in addition to general ambitions to record family events and children's performances, most participants had high expectations for their home video projects. This chapter examines why those ambitions were frequently disappointed and more generally why the camcorder was not used as often as anticipated by a majority of participants. We then discuss the kinds of uses that *were* achieved by the households and analyze the factors that enabled those particular uses, including their motivations for using the camcorder (and the resulting video footage). We conclude by considering the essentially private nature of home video, suggesting that its functions and meanings also need to be examined on a more personal or subjective level.

"PIE IN THE SKY"

Most of our participants set out with the aim of using the camcorder to create a record of family life and of significant events in their own and particularly their children's life course (thus fulfilling Chalfen's documentation, memory, and cultural membership functions). However, there were exceptions to this classic home mode genre. Jocelyn, in particular, at the beginning of the project said she wanted to do something "fun and creative" and had a "pie in the sky idea . . . of putting something together, of trying to do some filming and bits myself." Many children also had aims as video makers that were different from those of most adult participants (e.g., creating edited videos connected with popular music and mainstream feature films), while Edward, as a single retired person, had ambitions that extended beyond capturing family life and events and included semiprofessional activities (such as making videos to sell to tourists). Although the children took turns recording home mode material (generally taking over when the adults needed to do something, such as bring in the birthday cake), and Edward also recorded Christmas activities with his grandchildren at his daughter's house, for the most part the children and Edward were not recording family life as Chalfen describes. Later in the chapter, we analyze the kinds of video making that occurred and discuss how our data extends Chalfen's conception of the home mode. However, we need to begin by focusing on the first stages of the domestication of the camcorder—the commodification and appropriation stages.

As we discussed in chapter 1, the camcorder is framed by discourses within magazines, advertising, and mainstream media as a tool with which to create finished movies that can be easily shared with friends, family, and wider networks. This commodification of the camcorder clearly impacted our participants' ambitions. Throughout the project, many of them imagined producing edited movies for distribution. The products they envisaged creating included documentaries (which could be shared with a wider audience or in Edward's case sold to tourists), animations, various "creative" projects with children, MySpace music videos, "video postcards" (short videos to show snippets of everyday life), and "video albums" (similar to photo albums).

For some, these edited products were imagined as creative projects unto themselves, while for others the editing was simply about "taking out the boring bits" in order to make the videos more "watchable" by friends and family. Some also saw editing as a means of creating a kind of unified depository or archive of images about a particular family member or members (which they described as a video portfolio, scrapbook, or album). Aidan described his view of video scrapbooks as follows:

> I imagine it will be a video disc. With, you know, different little chapters of short bits that say "tenth birthday party," "summer holiday," whatever. So you can just select . . . or look through them one by one. And none of them are very long. So it's like looking through a photo album . . . with some longer ones edited together. But more like a sort of scrapbook.

Several participants echoed Aidan's aim of creating an organized and edited selection of videos, often for the children when they left home (in Shanta's case, for boarding school) and/or when they were older. There was a sense here of wanting to build and hold onto a coherent narrative of one's life, which would provide stability in what otherwise felt like a fast-moving and chaotic world. Drawing on Anthony Giddens's (1991) notion of "ontological security," Silverstone and colleagues (1992) argue that as part of the domestication of technology, households create narratives that sustain a sense of their own stability. New technologies can challenge or reinforce that security: mobile phones can disrupt the boundary between work and leisure time, for example, or they can provide reassuring links with family members away from home. This drive to generate ontological security can be seen to inform the ways in which technologies are integrated into households: it underlies the rules that are negotiated over their use (e.g., no text messaging at the dinner table) and the aspirations that people invest in them (e.g., creating a coherent and happy narrative for each child).

Importantly, these imagined uses also reflect particular forms of social and cultural capital. The participants who anticipated sharing videos with wider audiences were in a social position for that imaginary to be possible. Mariya, who had connections with government officials in the former Soviet republic of Georgia and whose husband worked in the field of educational technology, saw herself sharing videos with policy makers and online groups; Neil, Barney, and Phil, who all had accounts on MySpace and were involved with music groups of varying degrees of seriousness, imagined making music videos to post there; Shanta, who wanted to make video portfolios of her children reading the Quran in public competitions, discussed how these videos would be used as part of their applications to private boarding schools; Jocelyn, who worked in the creative industries and had watched her colleagues edit video, including producing edited family vacation videos for others, imagined herself doing something similar; and Edward, who was involved in a club for pensioners and had enjoyed some success as a photographer in a camera club, imagined making videos to share with pensioners who were housebound or to sell to people who were unable to travel to London. Interestingly, these more ambitious aspirations all move the camcorder to the conversion stage, where the meanings and values inscribed in the use of the camcorder are made public (Silverstone et al. 1992).

Certain participants saw the video as a tool to record a performance and then learn by reviewing and evaluating, a conscious connection with discourses regarding reflexivity and self-improvement (Giddens 1991) and the pedagogic function of parenting (Walkerdine and Lucey 1989). Bruno described this: "It's really very instructive. In fact, when we do it it's a very effective way of telling you what you do wrong, or with teaching or something. You see yourself as somebody else would." This usage related primarily to developing specific skills (public speaking, sports, or music), as well as general attitudes toward learning (starting and completing a project) and promoting progression and growth over time (particularly for children).

Many of the types of projects imagined by the participants involved transferring video from tape to another format and then editing, and often they would involve time, patience, organization, and technical skills. As we will see in chapter 5, in the end only Jocelyn and Yaron invested significant amounts of time and effort in producing an edited product. Yaron shared his video online but commented that he had doubts about the value of spending so many hours on such a project, given the lukewarm responses he received. At the end of our 15 months, Jocelyn was not satisfied enough with her edited piece to share it with her friends and family, and in fact she revised her ambitions in relation to the camcorder: when she first received it, she imagined using it to videotape scripted sketches and produce edited projects (as a "creative outlet"), but by the end of the project she had come to see it merely as a way to archive her family life. Her creative focus switched to screen writing, still with a possible aim of producing a show reel of sketches, but certainly not at the moment. As she said when we last met, "I'll have to get lots of footage of [the family reunion] and put that together. But then also moving on more with my creative projects."

This is not to say that participants were disappointed by the technology or did not achieve any of their aims. Many of the less ambitious (and perhaps more realistic) aims have yet to be discussed. Rather, the participants with high ambitions often revised or abandoned these ideas or projected them as future projects. In this respect, we could say that certain aspects of the camcorder never went past the appropriation stage and were never incorporated into the routines of the household. However, these aspects are primarily those advocated by the advertisements, magazines, and how-to-do-it books discussed in chapter 1, as well as ambitions informed by the previous experiences and social connections of the individual participants (e.g., watching videos on MySpace, seeing edited videos made by friends and colleagues). Later in this chapter, some of the participants' actual home mode video practices are analyzed, as we look more closely at the incorporation stage.

"LIFE GOT IN THE WAY"

In certain respects, all the camcorders moved to the incorporation stage: they became functional (i.e., almost all the households used them regularly over the 15 months), and they were fitted into the routines of the household (although the routine use of the camcorder may only have involved special occasions). However, there were several barriers that prevented participants from using it as they had originally envisioned. We can identify three main barriers here: time, interest, and technology.

Jocelyn remarked on how she started editing her footage, and then "life got in the way," which prevented her from finishing projects. This was a recurring theme, related not only to editing but also simply to getting the camcorder out of its storage space. Most obviously, in terms of projects involving editing, time was a major factor, as Nicole described: "just getting round to . . . do it really. So, having a bit of spare time to sit down and do it actually. Get everything out and plug it all in and get my son off the computer, which is hard work." At the end of the 15 months, many of the interviewees projected forward to a time when their children were older (or even when they themselves were retired) and they would have time to sort through the videos and make edited scrapbooks or compilations.

Another barrier was the lack of time to engage in projects involving the camcorder (e.g., setting something up to video) or even to engage in activities that one might want to videotape. Aidan and Bruno both described fitting in full-time work with hectic childcare arrangements during the week (which involved shuttling children to school, parties, and activities). Nicole described how her videotaping practically stopped when her daughter moved to secondary school and was no longer involved in competitions or performances (as she had been in primary school); furthermore, Nicole's financial situation changed so that the family had neither the time nor the financial resources to go on day trips or holidays, therefore reducing the number of occasions on which the camcorder might come out. Many of the participants apologized to us for not using the camcorder more often, and often in the interviews we heard about upcoming vacations when they anticipated having the time to use it. Nicole's comment is typical:

> It's just that work's been quite busy, and we haven't really been doing too much in this time of the year. So hopefully . . . we'll probably use it a lot more in the summer holidays, which will be nice.

All of these dimensions of nonuse point to potential motivations for using the camcorder that are analyzed further in the next section, although they also indicate the connection between financial resources and use.

A further barrier was when the camcorder was simply forgotten due to the other priorities involved in preparing for family outings or vacations. Aidan described the amount of preparation involved in going on a day trip with three children, with other needs such as food and dry clothing being a priority; Loren related how devastated she was when the camcorder was left behind (sitting out on a bed) when the family left on a big trip to Australia; Nicole noted how she forgot to recharge the battery before her daughter's trampolining competition.

Finally, videotaping involved having a spare set of hands—someone who was not involved in the action. This was most clear in Phil's description of not being able to make a video of his road trips because he was too busy navigating, but it also explains gendered patterns of use. In Leslie's case, when Matt was the video maker, she was the main person organizing food and preparations during family get-togethers; Phil described how he got the camcorder out during the 45 or so minutes when his partner was "faffing about" getting prepared to take the two young children out. Furthermore, there was a sense that videotaping involved taking time out from an activity or even stopping it completely, as Yaron described:

> We were sort of walking quite a lot, and we didn't really have time to stop and video. When we were in Israel on the beach, sitting down and relaxing in the same place more or less, it was kind of easier to fuss about with it.

Similarly, Leslie also commented that she found it hard to stop what she was doing in order to videotape, remarking that it had not yet become a "habit" beyond simply recording special occasions.

Clearly, the participants' "pie in the sky" projects demanded time, patience, and discipline—something that became clear to them over the course of the 15 months. Sustained interest and motivation were needed in order to achieve the kind of results they had originally imagined. Although many of the participants started more ambitious projects (skits, a video diary, music videos), these mostly remained as clips on the videotapes interspersed with other home mode video. Further, parents who imagined doing projects with their children soon discovered that the projects required sustained interest and did not provide the immediate rewards that children needed. Klaus, age 7, said this quite clearly: "It's boring to do the same thing all the time, just holding the camera." Yaron, who originally envisioned his children taking the camcorder and doing independent projects, remarked:

> They'll spend hours drawing, painting, making models and working with materials. And there . . . is satisfaction; it's so much more in proportion to their investment [than with video]. . . . They'll draw a picture, it'll come out nice, and they can show it to everyone the minute it's done.

This lack of immediate reward and the need for sustained interest and discipline might explain unfinished projects by other young people (e.g., Barney and Ted) who clearly had an interest and desire to produce video but never seemed to get around to completing a project.

A further barrier to use, particularly more ambitious use, was the technology itself. With participants who were not comfortable with technology, infrequent use exacerbated feelings of discomfort. Halfway through the project, Leslie remarked that she did not use the camcorder often enough to remember how to use it, though this had changed by the end of the project. There were varying degrees of technological barriers: for example, some people were unsure how to download the video to a computer or transfer it to a DVD or VHS tape, while others were fully aware of the procedures but recognized the limitations of transferring video to a hard drive (mainly space on the hard drive, but also concerns about reduction in quality). Again, time was a major factor here—even simply transferring to a DVD required a degree of organization and dedication.

At the end of the project, Yaron in particular had adjusted his ambitions and expectations for the camcorder, due to technical constraints. Here he speculated about the role of up-to-the-minute technology in the home:

> We just don't have the right kind of set-up. . . . I wonder if we had a good

high-powered Mac station at home then it's easy to download and edit. . . .
So if it were that easy to just throw something, off-load, edit it, almost in real
time, and then view it.

This fantasy of "instant creativity" is of course one that is strongly pro-
moted in the advertising for home computers, particularly Macs. Access
to a high-powered computer might have helped such people achieve their
aims, although Edward, who only had access to a computer through a
local community center, did far more videotaping than our other participants, who all had relatively new computers in their homes. Access to
the Internet was another technological barrier, and Jocelyn in particular
speculated that if she had access she would have had more incentive to
finish her editing projects for e-mailing to friends and family.

Often participants compared the ease of using still cameras (the video
function, as well as the still function) or the video function on camera
phones with the more cumbersome use of the camcorder. Yaron said
that video requires more sustained attention and thought (compared to a
quick snapshot on a still camera):

> You have to direct it, then you have to edit, and you have to think very well
> about where you position yourself and, and, not just spatially but also tem-
> porally. . . . You really have to kind of adapt your whole behavior to the fact
> that you are taking a video.

Several people said mobile phone cameras made sharing video much
easier, in contrast to the technological difficulties and the inconvenience
of sharing video from a camcorder. In Mikhael's case, he found it relatively easy to e-mail a video from a mobile phone, and he also commented
that a mobile phone was easier to fit into his life than a camcorder (due
to the portability and constant presence of the phone—see also Willett
2009). Neil also commented that the size of video files makes them less
convenient for sharing (in comparison with MP3s—this is in relation to
music videos). In Jocelyn's case, she also made a very impromptu video
on her mobile phone (of Jack riding his bike) to share with someone in
her office (the person who had given them the bike); again, this video
and the sharing of it would have been less likely if she had relied only on

the camcorder. Aidan also mentioned how camera phone video was used differently from camcorder video, with children recording impromptu embarrassing moments to pass around for immediate viewing. However, Mikhael noted that even mobile phone videos required downloading, labeling, organizing, and in some cases compressing. Several participants contrasted this with the ease of printing, organizing, and sharing photographs. Edward commented:

> You can't stick a video in a frame on the wall. . . . The movie is great, it outstrips statics, but you gotta have some equipment to show it. I couldn't bump into you in the street and say, "Oh, have a look at my latest film."

Finally, there were barriers relating to the social space. Neil said that his aim of videotaping different grime music events was hindered by tensions between the groups of people involved. Several participants commented on the risk of taking a camcorder out of the home, particularly when the video maker was a teenage boy. Loren commented, "I think it is particularly an issue because teenage boys are the ones who tend to get things taken from them, so everyone's alert." This might explain why almost all of the videos produced by the boys or young men in our study (Neil, Neil's brother, Ted, Barney, and Felix) were confined to home settings, apart from when the camcorder was part of a family outing or vacation. Several participants commented on fears of the camcorder being stolen (and in fact one was stolen) and not wanting to have the extra responsibility or hassle of having to worry about protecting it on family outings.

TOWARD A NEW TYPOLOGY OF HOME MODE VIDEO

From the analysis so far, it is clear that the incorporation stage involved various barriers and obstacles. The purpose of examining these barriers is not to highlight the failure of technology or to describe participants' disappointments. Rather, examining failed "high hopes" and barriers to those ambitions helps to highlight the construction of those ambitions, as well as practices that are more achievable and the factors that might enable those practices. We would argue that home mode video functions in ways that are different from those that are commonly discussed (or

More Private Practices   **More Public Practices**

⬅————————————————————————————————➡

Fig. 1. Home mode continuum

imagined), not only in how-to-do-it books and magazines but also by academic authors such as Ouellette (1995) and Zimmerman (1995). In line with Chalfen's work, we need to examine what is happening in people's everyday uses of the camcorder, rather than focusing on what is *not* happening.

As we have discussed, although Chalfen collected and analyzed his data over 20 years ago, and since then various technological developments have changed the experience of domestic video making, the content and functions of the home mode that he describes closely match the data from our study. However, we also found a range of practices that involve more *public* video making, learning, and sharing, which we might see as extensions of the home mode. The data we collected can be considered in relation to a continuum, with private practices on one end and public practices on the other (see fig. 1).

Whereas a majority of the videos Chalfen analyzed fall somewhere in the middle of the continuum, we have evidence of more "private" videos (e.g., Loren's video diary, footage of intimate family moments) and more "public" ones (e.g., Phil and Neil's videos for MySpace). Of course, we have not seen many of the very private videos, since they were by definition intended only for the individuals who made them, and perhaps for immediate family, while the public videos, as we have seen, were often aspirations rather than realities. Nevertheless, there is evidence here that a broader range of practices exists and that, importantly, there are connections on this continuum between the nature of the video content (private versus public) and the other themes we consider in subsequent chapters (both the subjective elements of video making and its role in developing "media literacy").

For example, more *private* video practices tend to involve videotaping for the purpose of self-reflection, personal enjoyment, or sharing with a very small group of family members or friends, whereas more *public* practices tend to involve videotaping for the purpose of communicating with a wider audience. In terms of identity, participants who video mainly for more private purposes tend to see themselves as family archivists rather than as video makers; whereas participants who are more publicly oriented seem more comfortable taking on the identity of a "serious" video maker. And in terms of learning and film grammar, private practices tend to be less concerned with components such as composition, editing, or even lighting, whereas public practices tend to involve a more developed form of media literacy.

A further consideration here is how the continuum reflects gendered patterns of use. Distinctions between private and public practices are typically discussed in terms of gender, with women occupying more private spaces and men dominating more public spaces (e.g., Fraser 1992; McRobbie 1978). However, our data complicates this distinction: we have women who take the camcorder out of the home to record their children's public performances and men who record intimate family moments within the home. This might be seen to reflect the fluidity—or even the shifting patterns—of gendered identities more broadly.

Most of our households did not sit at any one point on this continuum, partly because there were often several video makers in one household who had different styles of use and different purposes for videotaping, but also because individual participants each had a range of video making practices. Edward, for example, made a private video of his family at Christmas, which he shared only with his daughter and her family, and he also made a video of his pensioners' club's Christmas dinner, which he then showed to the entire club. Ten-year-old Ted recorded himself lip-synching to pop songs and also took over the camcorder at public events such as school discos. Therefore, rather than giving a label to each household that might summarize their place on this continuum, the next section outlines the different styles of use and purposes for videotaping which we encountered across the households. We have divided the participants' video making practices into three broad categories: event recording, everyday recording, and performances for the camera. These three categories incorporate various functions, as well as different degrees of privacy and skill connected with video making.

Event Recording

Many of the videos we watched were of special events related to the family. These include family vacations or outings; children's performances (school plays, competitions, sporting events); and birthday and holiday celebrations (private events in the home [opening presents in pajamas] and more public parties). For some households, event recording was the primary function of the camcorder, which otherwise rarely came out of its storage space. Similarly, some people identified themselves as event recorders more than others in the household. For example, Aidan said that he used the camcorder mainly for parties, performances, and outings, whereas his children engaged in various types of playful activity connected with videotaping; Nicole said her children recorded various "silly" things (their grandmother interacting with a cat), whereas she was more focused on capturing important family events; Shanta said, "I'm not the type of person to walk around and . . . record for the sake of it" (although she said her husband described her videotaping as "messing around"). Finally, Jocelyn contrasted her style of videotaping with less purposeful types: "I do use it for projects. Specific projects. I don't really carry it around on spec."

Events were sometimes videotaped to share with people who could not attend (working parents, friends, or relatives who lived some distance away) and were shared in a variety of ways. The most private kinds of event sharing were with parents who could not attend children's performances—in this case the video was watched soon after the event in the privacy of the home. Similarly, event videos were sometimes watched by friends and relatives who visited the homes. More public sharing involved transferring recordings (to DVDs or VHS tapes) and passing the recordings around to friends and family. Thus, in addition to sharing the pensioners' Christmas dinner video, Edward shared his video of the reopening of St. Pancras train station with his photography club (this was transferred unedited to a DVD); at the end of our project, Jocelyn was almost ready to share her carefully edited vacation videos (via e-mail); Shanta told us that her family had a tradition of passing around videos of children's performances; and Yaron edited a video of a family outing, uploaded it to a video sharing site, and sent the link to friends and relatives (the video was set as private on the site). On our home mode continuum, therefore, we found a range of practices connected with event recording involving different audiences, purposes, technologies, and techniques. However, even the most public of these practices (sharing online or with a club) were still in many ways private.

The functions of event recording vary and clearly align with the functions outlined by Chalfen (documentary, memory, and cultural membership). In terms of documentary, recording events is partly a matter of creating a personal visual history and of validating relationships (documenting the events themselves, as well as who was there). As Aidan suggested, there were many similarities here between videos and photo albums. As we discuss in the following chapter, event recording also functions in terms of memory—as a way to "repeat and re-experience . . . pleasurable times" (Chalfen 1987, 138–39). Our participants saw video as particularly effective in evoking memories, as it captures sound and movement, not just the still image as in a photograph. Finally, event recording functions to confirm cultural membership—"the visual display of proper and expected behavior, of participation in socially approved activities, according to culturally approved value schemes" (139). This final function is particularly true for Shanta, who mainly wanted the camcorder to record her children's participation in competitions involving reading the Quran, the videos then passed around to various family members, shown at family gatherings, and potentially used as part of a portfolio application for private religious schools. Obviously, with participants who were mainly event recorders, the more events in which a household was involved, the more the camcorder was used, and as discussed earlier in relation to barriers, the lack or reduction of such events (due to financial circumstances or simply changes in children's public activities due to age) accounted for a decrease in camcorder use or its lack of incorporation into the household.

Everyday Recording

Although our analysis supports Chalfen's assertion that not every facet of daily life is recorded, many of the participants in our study recorded less eventful and more everyday aspects of family life than the celebrations and outings described above. Such videos included meals (particularly young children at mealtime), children playing (alone or with other children, inside the home or garden, or at public playgrounds), and adults and children interacting (e.g., reading aloud or preparing food). Here the participants explicitly discussed wanting to capture the everyday dynamics and interactions between friends and family members or the character and personality of their children at a particular age (before they grew up). In this context, participants talked about realism as the desired aesthetic—wanting to capture people unawares and interacting naturally.

> Phil: I'm using it . . . sort of spontaneously . . . when they're being funny or something. Or when they're not aware that I've got it on and it's sort of a naturalistic way.

More covert techniques were sometimes used here: Matt talked about videotaping his children through a doorway, and Edward said he sometimes closes the LCD screen so that it does not look as if he is videotaping.

In contrast with the style of use connected with event recording, participants who recorded more everyday video described their use of the camcorder as casual and spontaneous (as we see in the excerpt above from Phil), particularly in comparison with their partner:

> Mariya (e-mail): I am more casual than my husband about its use. . . . I think his criteria of "worthwhileness" of the filming is tougher than mine.

Children also recorded everyday activities, often by simply picking up the camcorder and walking around their homes. Family pets were popular here, as were computer and television screens. This practice sometimes turned into surveillance-type situations, as the video makers tried to sneak up on family members and capture, among other things, an older sister on the computer, an older brother in the bathroom preparing to go out, or adults' private conversations. Referring to the constant presence of the camcorder, 11-year-old Joe called himself "the paparazzi," and both Mariya and Neil described their camcorder as similar to having CCTV in their home. The presence of everyday recording might have been related to the number of video tapes available to the participants (not feeling the need to economize on tape and/or feeling the need to fill tapes for the purposes of the research). This also depended on how often experiences were repeated—regular visits to the park or to grandmother's house, for example, meant that the "special" events (feeding the ducks) did not need to be recorded during every visit, and therefore more everyday and intimate interactions were recorded (everyday conversations with grandmother).

Everyday recording also included an anthropological approach, wanting to record elements of a place as a kind of cultural record. This was clearly one of Neil's aims when he applied to be on the project: his application stated that he wanted "to give an insight into life in WC1." In some cases this was a relatively private practice. For example, Shanta recorded images of Bangladesh, particularly scenes from where she had lived as a child (fields, swimming places, her school), as a record for her children who had not been there. Mariya also said she recorded everyday things that might remind the children of their time in London when they moved back to Georgia (squirrels, particular foods, the apartment). For some participants, however, everyday recording was for a wider purpose. Mariya, in particular, discussed recording everyday elements of Western culture that might be useful for sharing with people in Georgia in order to influence cultural change (e.g., videos of procedures in schools or openly gay couples on the street). Edward also recorded everyday scenes in London, describing his approach in anthropological terms. Here he describes a video of a particular bus journey that went through different neighborhoods of London:

> And you see different houses, different gardens. And it gets in to the East End where you see men in little shops, Bangladeshi shops. And people in different dress. It gets up to the city and then you see pinstripe and bowler hat, umbrella. And it goes through banks and big businesses. And then it gets out the other side. You go through Oxford Street where there's a mixture, everybody shopping. Then you go to Baker Street and you change again to people sort of well-dressed and visitors and tourists. So, you've gone through the whole lot of different types of people.

Although the content can be described as everyday, the videos in this category display a range of techniques and skills. In terms of media literacy or video technique, Edward's recordings can be described as more artistic or creative than other home mode practices: he is more careful about light, sound, and framing, and in interviews he expressed his interest in the aesthetic qualities of filmmaking (see chapter 5)—and, as we have noted, he also expressed the wish to become a professional video maker.

The purposes of this kind of everyday video making also varied. While Edward wanted to document London life, possibly to show to people abroad or to those who were not able to travel to or around London, much of this fits more easily into the functions discussed in relation to event recording (Chalfen's documentary, memory, and cultural membership functions). Everyday recordings might be seen to provide more evidence within each of these categories. "The everyday" by definition is less of a performance than an event and therefore is in some ways more authentic as a form of documentary. Relationships are also being documented here on a more personal level (e.g., everyday conversations between children and their grandparents). The material for future memories is more detailed and naturalistic (e.g., showing how Leslie and Matt's two daughters played with their Barbie dolls). Cultural membership is about not only public display but also intimate private moments (e.g., a mother breast-feeding her baby). In terms of incorporating the camcorder into the household, for some participants, recording the everyday was a new and unexpected pleasure; it was particularly striking that two fathers (Mahaz and Mikhael) found that the camcorder came to function most purposefully for them when they were recording everyday events. Mahaz's recording of scenes from his hometown in Bangladesh, and Mikhael's of his wife and daughter in the kitchen, were described by them as being among the few occasions when they had actually enjoyed video making.

Performances for the Camcorder

As we saw with the "pie in the sky" ambitions discussed in the earlier section, the camcorder was also seen by some as a tool for creative practice. Jocelyn, Bruno, Mariya, Loren, and Yaron all anticipated doing creative projects with the camcorder; although after seeing how video making fitted (or did not fit) into family routines, and experiencing the technology as more cumbersome in terms of transferring and editing, they all adjusted their expectations. In several instances, we were also told of children preparing to be videotaped (working up a sketch or dance routine) but then losing interest when it came to actually getting out the camcorder. However, a significant proportion of the video data from the project can be classified as "performances for the camcorder"—activities that are sometimes part of what is already happening but are nevertheless performed specifically for videotaping. These were generally private performances, done in the home either alone or with friends and family. (Interestingly, in Chalfen's analysis of home mode content, he did not find people performing for the home movie camera in this way.)

Yaron produced a video of a staged conversation between his children that was presented as part of a compilation video at a wedding reception. However, beyond this, there were few examples of such performance projects coming to fruition (i.e., being produced as finished pieces). More typical were instances of playful sketches and performances in front of the camcorder that were interspersed among the event and everyday video footage. Phil started several comedy sketches, including one in which he was videotaped repeatedly taking out the trash to the rubbish chute over several days and one in which he performed skits related to letters of the alphabet with his 4-year-old daughter. Neil's brother videotaped a short session of himself rapping, and Jocelyn attempted some scripted skits.

In several other instances, however, the camcorder was part of children's play. At times it functioned as a prop or a mirror for play (or in some cases, as mentioned above, as an incentive to work on a skit or dance routine). Thirteen-year-old Barney recorded himself wrestling with a friend, followed by a "kitchen torture" game in which one person was tied to a chair, blindfolded, and fed "mystery" foods; Aidan's sons pretended to be sports commentators as they videotaped staged football matches; several videos across the households included lip-synching to pop songs or karaoke sets; Rachel (age 5) presented a dance routine to a Spice Girls song; and finally, Bruno helped stage a piano performance, with his son Klaus pretending to play a Scott Joplin rag. One particularly prolific playful video maker was 10-year-old Ted, whose video footage included staged action pieces for future edited productions of *Jaws, Mis-*

laid (after the TV series *Lost*), *Doctor Who,* and advertisements for Nike, as well as general playful performances for the camera, particularly with his younger sister.

In relation to our continuum, although these videos were made in private spaces and all except one remained largely unseen, there was a range of private and public practices (or at least intentions) here. Barney's wrestling and Rachel's dance videos were private, whereas Yaron was producing his children's video for more public consumption (a wedding reception), and the intention with the various music videos was to make them public on MySpace. More significant, however, is the media literacy or video technique aspect connected with these more public videos. Public performance videos involve an understanding of editing and continuity (Ted's aim was eventually to edit all the bits of footage together), and more developed skills and understanding are seen as necessary if one wants to go public. (This might in turn explain why a vast majority of home videos remain private.)

An important aspect of these performances for the camcorder was how they functioned in terms of Chalfen's cultural membership category. For young people in particular, the culture they were connecting with was more peer-centered than in traditional home mode video. Barney and Neil (as well as Neil's brother) aimed to make grime music videos, and as mentioned above, several of Ted's videos were connected with popular media texts (songs, TV shows, and advertisements). While these performances were often part of family events and everyday play, they were functioning in additional ways by asserting forms of cultural membership or knowledge that went beyond the family.

Given the amount of performance video we saw from children in the study, we can conclude that there was considerable pleasure in having the camcorder act as a mirror or perhaps a secret or private viewer for their performances. When children planned skits or dance routines to be videotaped, the activities often relied on popular media (e.g., Ted's various homage videos, Barney's wrestling video, and Rachel's Spice Girls dance routine). John Fiske (1987) discusses the pleasures involved in playing with media texts—which serve as a way both of appropriating new identities (Rachel perhaps imagined herself as an older girl or even a Spice Girl) and also of controlling roles and representations through the ways in which they are performed (Rachel's routine featured gymnastics rather than sexual innuendo). Through this kind of pleasurable play with texts, roles and representations are chosen and can be replicated, but equally they can be subverted, negotiated, or resisted.

One further characteristic of performances for the camera was the role of this use in the domestication of the camcorder. In some cases, we might hypothesize that the placement of the camcorder (part of the objectification stage) made a difference in its use for performance, particularly in children's play. Those households that had the camcorder out in the domestic space more regularly seemed to generate more performances: thus, we had the impression that Aidan and Ted's camcorder (which was used most frequently in this category) was always at hand and rarely put away in a cupboard. However, simply having a camcorder easily available did not in itself cause children to perform: various other factors contributed to this, including (in this case) the ages of the children and Ted's previous interest in videotaping. Obviously, the more uses the participants saw for the camcorder, the more it was incorporated into the household. In terms of the incorporation stage, then, performances for the camcorder added another purpose for videotaping, thus leading to greater presence of the camcorder, greater comfort in being behind and in front of the camera, and generally greater integration into the routines of the household. This was clear in Aidan's description of Ted's camcorder projects:

> The project is sort of an adjunct to whatever they're playing. And when we were on holiday and him and Luke and Max were playing football in the garden, they kind of filmed bits of them playing and then watched it and commentated on it.

MOTIVATING AND ENABLING VIDEO MAKING

As discussed in the previous section on participants' ambitions for video making, their "pie in the sky" ideas were partly framed by the commercial rhetoric surrounding the commodification of the camcorder. Given that most of these ambitions were disappointed, we need to look further to see why people did actually use the camcorders. This section examines participants' motivations for video making and also the factors that enabled their use. The motivations connected with memory and emotion will be discussed in much more detail in chapter 4, while the theme of motivation in relation to learning is addressed in chapter 5.

The event and everyday recordings discussed in the previous section were essentially motivated by a desire to share events and daily life, often with friends and family (though Edward had a different audience in mind), and to develop a family archive (again, Edward's archive was for a different audience). All our participants had friends or relatives whom they saw as an audience for their videos. Often their audiences were in other countries, but they also included elderly people living nearer who were unable to travel to or around London or were uncomfortable making the journey. There was a particular motivation to record things for family members who were unable to be at an event (including school performances, as well as experiences such as skiing). However, there was also a motivation to show friends and family a picture of daily life—the children growing up, the place they were living, or in the case of Edward, a walk or bus ride through parts of London. To take just one example, Jocelyn (with her 6-year-old son Jack) had parents in Hong Kong and brothers in Australia and wanted to record daily routines, as well as more eventful occasions, in the forms of "day-in-the-life videos" and "postcard videos" to share with them. Like other participants, she said that part of the motivation was to keep in touch with her family, for Jack to get to know his cousins, and for her parents to see what their life in London was like. Perhaps because of this motivation, Jocelyn produced everyday recordings (fly-on-the wall videos of Jack playing or reading, preparations at mealtimes, Jack doing craft projects), as well as event recordings (vacations, birthdays, parties). Although Jocelyn was initially motivated by her distant audience, by the end of the project she had adjusted her aims and described herself more as a family archivist. Here, the motivation was simply to "to keep getting him while he's young" and to have a record for both of them. This motivation to capture memories of children as they grow up is addressed further in chapter 4.

As discussed in the section on ambitions, wider audiences also motivated some of the participants. Edward had a very immediate audience in his two clubs, and he also imagined an audience of other people who were interested in London (people who knew London and were no longer able to travel, tourists who would like to know more about the city). Significantly, Edward was not interested in joining a video making club, perhaps because his motivation was not to learn skills such as editing, but rather to share his videos with non–video makers. Mariya was also motivated by a wider audience, both online (a Facebook group connected with her degree and special interest groups) and face to face (policy makers in Georgia); the musicians (Phil, Barney, and Neil) imagined an audience on MySpace. Notably, only the immediate, known audiences (family for most, existing clubs for Edward) provided sufficient incentive for such sharing to actually happen.

The motivations for children and young people to make videos were often different. As described above, several children used the camcorder as part of their play: as a mirror, a prop, or a reason for play. Furthermore, videotaping functioned more in relation to membership in their peer culture than membership in a family culture. For children, the incorporation stage was partly determined by age—older children had more access to the camcorder and were better able to handle the technology than the younger children in our study. Mariya commented that her 7-year-old daughter was afraid of breaking the camcorder and found it difficult to hold with her small hands. However, this was not the case with Klaus (also age 7). Furthermore, in Aidan's household, the middle child, Ted, used the camcorder far more than the older child, although Yaron's son, who was the same age as Ted, was not nearly as motivated to use the camcorder. More important, perhaps, was how the camcorder fitted in with existing play. Barney's wrestling video recorded something that was already happening, as did the karaoke videos and a video Lexi made of her friends playing Truth or Dare. Obviously, performance-related play of this kind lends itself to videotaping more than other kinds of play.

In looking at what kinds of video making occurred, it is clear that having an audience or a context for production can help one get past the initial appropriation stage. In the case of Matt and Leslie, the camcorder was incorporated into their household reasonably unproblematically for a variety of reasons, but partly because of audience and context. Matt regularly left recordings with his mother, whom they visited every month, as well as with Leslie's Irish family. The camcorder allowed Matt to fulfill a particular role as a son and brother-in-law/uncle—as the technologically competent one who helped maintain family connections partly through video. As a father and husband, he also had a role connected with the camcorder—to keep an archive of his family, particularly the children growing up. Matt also had an interest in technology and had friends who were semiprofessional filmmakers. Finally, he had also grown up with Super 8 filmmaking and reflected on how this provided a model for home video making:

> My father used to use Super 8. . . . The film was like two minutes, so you had to be more careful when you used it. That's why he likes Super 8s because they can be more interesting to watch because people are always doing something interesting.

Although it took some months for Leslie to be comfortable with the camcorder, by the end of the 15 months, she was happy to videotape school functions (her stated aim), and her 6-year-old daughter, Rachel, reminded Leslie to bring the camcorder to record such events. Videotaping had become such a functional aspect of their household that Rachel was making videos of her dolls with her own still camera.

One of the enabling factors in the incorporation stage of any technology is motivation and purpose, but there are also factors concerned with how the technology fits with daily life. With Leslie and Matt, the family already had roles in which there was space for the camcorder, or as Leslie jokingly commented, "That's why we've got Matt. It feels like he's responsible for [the camcorder]." Matt was the family expert on technology (Leslie said she did not even know how to work the satellite TV), and he pursued technology as part of his musical hobby, thus already making time to focus on media production. As a result, he was more relaxed with the camcorder, adding it to his interactions with the children, whereas Leslie felt it disrupted her interactions with her children and therefore recorded only formal events (school assemblies where she was already sitting in the audience).

Many participants indicated that recording and watching video footage became part of family outings or vacations, and certainly we watched a great deal of this kind of footage. This aligned with comments that videotaping happened when participants had more time to devote to both family activities and the use of technology. As a result of this practice, Aidan said that Ted's future edited video of *Jaws* would contain all the beaches they had visited in the past couple of years. Viewing video was also connected with family vacations. Yaron described how sharing video became part of retelling an event:

> We would, say, go somewhere in the morning and take a video, and then in the afternoon or the next day we would sit with people and just connect the camera directly to the TV and say, "Oh look, this is where we went yesterday and seen." So it had become part of recounting the event.

In the case of Leslie and Matt's family, Matt would leave very roughly edited VHS videos with family in Ireland and England; particularly for the children (cousins) who were playing together in Ireland, these videos became popular viewing, perhaps as part of reexperiencing, recounting, and remembering their time together: Leslie commented, "The girls have a cousin who then misses them dreadfully, so [she] puts it on and watches them all the time, which is quite nice."

As in Matt's case, the incorporation of camcorders depended partly on previous experience and existing skills and interests. Existing social networks and skills were discussed earlier in this chapter in relation to ambitions (e.g., envisioning music videos to post on MySpace). However, we saw more concrete examples in relation to actual video making practices. In Nicole's household, Nicole and her older son were the main video makers, and they explained how Nicole's husband showed little interest in technology, whereas Nicole works as an ICT trainer. Aidan presented himself as media literate (e.g., discussing various cinematic techniques), and he was clearly comfortable with technology (e.g., happily installing a USB card onto his hard drive). This experience and interest enabled him to work with Ted to explain techniques related to editing (see chapter 5). Edward's experience of videotaping was closely connected with his experience of photography: he entered (and was successful in) photo competitions, had sold his photographic work, and even had business cards with an artistic pseudonym. On a more practical level, he was part of a photography club (which incorporated video), and he received press passes for events through the club. Edward certainly had experiences and networks that enabled him to see himself as a "serious" video maker and also to make and share videos with a wider audience.

One final aspect that facilitated incorporation into households was the particular affordance of video in contrast with still photographs. Several participants were motivated to use the camcorder because of the capacity to capture more action and emotion: the "full spectrum," in Mariya's words; the "secret behind the photo," as Neil put it; a "sense of life and the variations" for Ruba. Others mentioned being able to capture more of people's personalities and more of the whole person, which was particularly desirable with children, whose personalities were seen to be changing. Furthermore, video was seen to allow people to relax because the recording was happening for an extended period (rather than a snapshot), thus achieving the desirable naturalistic feel and in some ways a more accurate portrayal of a person. Most obviously, video was useful for capturing sound and movement (performances), as well as a greater sense of a whole place.

IS IT ALL HAPPY FAMILIES?

The following chapter considers the role of video in constructing family narratives. Certainly the functions proposed by Chalfen, which on the whole fit well with the material from our research, suggest that there is a particular construction of "happy families" in much of our data. As we have seen in chapter 1, it is this aspect that has attracted so much criticism from academic commentators on family video making. Yet one might well ask, why would families not want to construct this image of themselves? As Nicole describes:

> You're in a happy frame of mind and you're going out on an outing with your family and you want to record the happier moments. You don't want to be, like, just showing things that are really depressing. Because you've got no interest in filming anything 'cause it's a part of real life that you probably want to forget.

As this chapter has shown, video making has to fit in with particular aspects of family life: there needs to be someone available who has time and motivation to use the camcorder, and the camcorder is far more likely to be used when there is a specific purpose for videotaping (e.g., celebrations, performances, or vacations). All of these circumstances are more likely to generate a narrative of the happy family.

There are also particular reasons for *not* recording parts of domestic life. Primarily, the participants agreed that long, boring, or repetitive sequences were not desirable, and they either envisioned editing out those sections or said they were becoming more selective when videotaping. In a sense, they recognized that videos represented "highlights" of days and events, beyond the tedium and routine that actually constitute daily life. Furthermore, participants were particularly protective of private moments in relation to their video making. Loren was not comfortable sharing her video diary, which was about a very difficult time in her life; Neil was unwilling to show us the videos he recorded of his mother and sister having verbal and physical fights (although he did share these with friends). It is notable that these instances of extremely private video run counter to happy family narratives. Furthermore, these videos were discussed by both Loren and Neil in pedagogic or therapeutic terms—as something to look back on and learn from, as reflections of where they used to be, and as proof that they had moved on.

As we will see in the following chapter, seeing oneself on screen can evoke feelings of embarrassment, and videotaping is also sometimes about capturing embarrassing moments. Several participants discussed the importance of maintaining the privacy of such footage, and (as discussed earlier) even footage that was shared with wider networks still remained relatively private. These comments by Yaron demonstrate some of the reasons for selectively recording family life, as well as concerns about the privacy of video recordings:

The kids having tantrums is something which I probably wouldn't shoot. Well, first because . . . I think at that point, they need my support, and not having me as a sort of remote, detached observer. But also I think . . . that's kind of something which five years down the line might be very embarrassing for them. You know, if one of their friends finds and puts it on TV or something.

	More Private Practices		More Public Practices
	◄───►		
Content	diaries, private family events private play	children's performances	music videos, public events
Purposes	personal, theraputic	sharing	communication, artistic expression, group activity
Audience	self or intimate relations	large groups of friends/relatives	online or public groups
Identity	not a video maker	comfortable with technology	artist, serious video maker
Literacy	unconcerned with film grammar; no interest in or ambition to edit	basic techniques in relation to light, panning, zooming, sound, etc.; aims to edit or edits roughly	media literate; will edit

Fig. 2. Home mode continuum with examples of practice

Returning to our home mode continuum, it seems that our participants' videos are neither entirely public nor perceived as completely private. At the risk of being too schematic, we can chart our participants' practices on a continuum, according to different themes that have arisen from the data (see fig. 2).

Some of the components in figure 2 extend Chalfen's findings, particularly at the more public end of the continuum. These latter examples might be seen as instances of Silverstone, Hirsch, and Morley's (1992) conversion phase, in that the participants' aspirations for the camcorder involve sharing meanings related to home video with the "outside world." Yet while one might predict that new technologies connected with camcorders are making this aspect of conversion much more accessible, in actuality we rarely saw this happen. In our study, the outside world was also entirely limited to friends and family who were in the same cultural networks and who were likely to already share values connected with the videos. In this sense, conversion—displaying videos and sharing meaning with others—functioned in Chalfen's terms in relation to already established cultural memberships; to this extent, it remains a relatively conservative process, in which existing meanings are being reinforced rather than challenged. In some ways, this supports Zimmerman's (1995) critique of home video: the creative and political potential of the camcorder is lost in homes, and instead home video is bound to reinforce relatively traditional forms of "familialism." However, as we discuss in the following chapter, home mode video also functions on a personal level in very powerful ways, which are by no means inevitably conservative or reactionary. A necessary degree of ontological security, a sense of trust in the world as it should be, is secured through home video making, both during the act of videotaping and in the reviewing and sharing of the videos, not only in the present but also in the future that is yet only imagined.

CHAPTER 4

The Subject of Video

This chapter focuses on the affective properties of home video making and its role in relation to emotion, memory, and personal identity. As we indicated in chapter 3, many of the participants involved in our research used their video cameras primarily to keep a record of family life. In such cases, the desire to freeze time and preserve special moments, and the emotional investments placed in video footage, are often particularly clear. However, this chapter is not limited to a discussion of family-centered video but also looks at the wider range of video making practices we found in our 12 households.

Drawing on work informed by psychoanalysis, feminism, and cultural studies more broadly, we aim to unpack some of the emotional dimensions of home mode video making, including its role in the construction of subjectivity—that is, the "sense of self" that was articulated by the participants involved in our study. Following poststructuralist theory, we consider the self not as a coherent, unified, and bounded essence, but as an unstable, incomplete work-in-progress. Not all such "work" on the self can be considered to be rationally or consciously executed. We therefore draw on certain psychoanalytic approaches that look at the construction of self within the realms of the unconscious and the imaginary. From this perspective, we view home mode video making as, among other things, a means by which particular (socially celebrated and/or psychologically necessary) fictions are reiterated and reinforced. This stress on fiction, however, does not refer to something that is separate or separable from fact. Rather, it reflects the idea that fantasy and the imaginary are central forces in the construction of our sense of self. The consequences (the social, visceral, and psychological effects) of this are no less real than those of conscious, rational thought. Stuart Hall writes:

> Identities arise from the narrativization of the self, but the necessarily fictional nature of this process in no way undermines its discursive, material or political effectivity, even if the belongingness, the "suturing into the story" through which identities arise is partly in the imaginary (as well as the symbolic) and therefore, always, partly constructed in fantasy, or at least within a fantasmatic field. (1996, 4)

The chapter is split into two interrelated parts, both of which tackle issues of fantasy, belonging, and representation. The first part focuses on participants' experiences of the actual hands-on practice of video making: how it feels to be the video maker, how it feels to be videotaped, and the different positions people take up when they engage in these activities. Our main focus here is on the "phenomenology" of video making—the immediate experience of doing it—and particularly on its emotional dimensions. The second part of the chapter moves on to consider the material that people record, its functions in terms of memory and identity, and the emotional significance they attach to it. This distinction between the two parts of the chapter might be framed in terms of the "double articulation" mentioned in the previous chapter (Silverstone et al. 1992): the first part addresses aspects of the practice of video making itself, while the second deals with the meanings attached to it.

PART I: A PHENOMENOLOGY OF VIDEO MAKING

As was illustrated in the previous chapter, a variety of video making practices emerged in the study. These ranged from private practices such as diary making, play, and the recording of private family events, to more public practices such as recording musical performances and capturing footage of public spaces around the city. As we have noted, there are many crossovers between these more private and more public practices. Neither individuals nor households involved in this study can be completely fixed at any one point on our continuum. Participants like Edward or Mariya who seemed particularly interested in the more public dimensions—and in sharing their work with a wider audience—also used video in more personal and private ways. And despite the fact that many participants said that they wanted to have a camcorder primarily to video their children, a host of different ways of doing and understanding this emerged.

Another way of looking at this would be to consider the "subject positions" taken up by participants—that is, the ways in which they identified themselves with particular discourses or definitions of the practice of amateur video making. So, one might see oneself as a "creative" video maker, a "documentary" video maker, a "playful" video maker, or a "personal" video maker, who is generally uninterested in the medium and the technology and is simply concerned with making unstructured personal keepsakes. The participants in our study include "artists" who view their practice as a form of creative expression, involving a concern for the lighting, sound, and "feel" of their footage; playful "experimenters," who are keen to explore the camcorder's potential in terms of a range of media genres and styles; "facilitators," who present themselves as encouraging parents enabling their children to explore and express themselves with the camcorder; "family record keepers," who see their footage constituting something very similar to the traditional family photo album; "social record keepers," who, like family record keepers, express an interest in preserving something whose significance lies in future viewing; and so on.

As we have indicated, all of these positions are fluid and mutable. Overlaps exist, and changes take place over time. We have, for example, the more "creative" family record keeper like Yaron, who said that he wanted to "capture the essence of an event" and who tried to keep his footage "natural-looking." We have the family record keepers like Phil or Aidan, who were happy to play around and experiment with the camcorder, exploring a range of viewing angles (as Phil did) or playing around by mimicking or spoofing different media genres (as Aidan did with his sons). We have participants like Mariya, who was keen to collect both social *and* family records. We have the "facilitator" like Bruno, eager to enable his son to express himself with the camcorder, while also using it to collect family records. And we have participants like Jocelyn, who worked with her son toward the production of short experimental videos, while she also collected footage for "day-in-the-life" videos and "postcards" to send to her extended family.

Where such crossovers are evident in the intentions, approaches, and styles of different participants, their positions are more fixed in relation to their feelings about actually engaging with the camcorder itself. Again, there was a range of positions here: participants tended either to enjoy, to strongly dislike, or to feel generally relaxed about being behind the camera (as the one videotaping) and being in front of the camera (as the one being videotaped). Reactions to these two situations did not shift greatly over the period of the project. Generally, participants who enjoyed operating the camera at the start of the project tended to continue enjoying this, although there was obviously some gradual wearing-off of the novelty—and indeed, for one participant, Yaron, the practice had become "boring" by the end of the project. Likewise, participants who did *not* enjoy seeing themselves on screen at the start of the project tended to remain this way, although for some participants, this became easier as time went on.

Behind the Camera

How it feels to be behind the camera as the person videotaping is related to the ways in which participants understand the point of what they are doing. Often, where family record keeping is the primary purpose, little attention is paid to the aesthetic or technical quality of footage. The main point is capturing a particularly significant person or place: it is the content that matters rather than the form. One participant, Leslie, illustrates this position clearly. She simply wanted footage of particular people and events to keep, review, and show to others. She expressed little concern for the style or quality of her footage. Indeed, the actual practice of videotaping was entirely secondary to simply having the footage. She pointed out early on in the project, "Well basically [videotaping our children] is all we use it for, to be honest . . . any kind of family occasions."

Leslie stressed that her footage was collected purely for having memories of her daughters. She pointed out on several occasions that it was her husband, Matt, who actually enjoyed the practice. Leslie said he "just gets more into it." In contrast, in relation to her own practice, she said, "To be honest, sometimes it's a bit of a grief, it's like, oh, I don't want to carry that round."

For Leslie, however, it was not simply the practical problems involved in videotaping or her self-consciousness about being videotaped (which is discussed in the next section) that gave her "grief." She was one of several participants who suggested that they felt uncomfortably self-conscious about using the camcorder. This was either because it was seen to draw unwanted attention to the video maker or because using the camcorder was seen to somehow cut them off from the events being filmed. Indeed, virtually all of the adult participants agreed that being behind the camcorder somehow removed them from the action. However, this removal was experienced in significantly different ways by different participants. For some, it was seen as a bit of a nuisance or as entailing an withdrawal of the self that was in some way uncomfortable or undesirable. This was particularly true of parents who described filming their children. Leslie, for example, made the following comments about collecting footage of her children at Christmas:

> I think that's why I passed it over to him [indicating her husband]. He was doing it, which meant that I could enjoy the children opening their Christmas presents and all that kind of stuff while he was videoing them.

Bruno made a similar point, saying that "when you do a video you feel like you're less taking part." Yaron also referred to this sense of removal from the event being videotaped. For this reason, he felt that his still camera was better suited to recording certain occasions. He explained:

> It's more portable, but it's also less intrusive. I found that, for instance, at some of their school assemblies, I decided not to take the camcorder because I noticed, when I take the camcorder, I'm not actually looking at the event. And I actually miss the event because I'm focused on the camera. And with stills it doesn't happen because you take it out at one point, and then you put it back in your pocket.

Another participant, Loren, found that videotaping with her camcorder's LCD screen open provided a solution to this problem. She said this was a less "invasive" way of capturing events and allowed her to feel connected to the action:

> I find that [the LCD screen] does make you feel less like you're hidden behind the camera, doesn't it? It makes you feel more involved, doesn't it? It's quite good, that. . . . Well, when I was doing the wedding thing, I felt like it was rude to be like this [indicates holding the camcorder in front of her face], but somehow I didn't feel it was rude to have it like that [indicates holding the camcorder at chest level], because then I could still engage with people.

If certain participants perceived this feeling of removal or withdrawal as a negative thing, others saw it much more positively. Neil, for example, used the camcorder to videotape conflicts between his mother and sister. He said he showed this footage to them later to illustrate how foolish they looked. However, Neil also pointed out that both his mother and sister "love an audience" and that at points, they would deliberately place themselves within the view of the camcorder and "up the action" when they knew that they were being videotaped. Likewise, for Edward (the most obvious "social record keeper" of our participants), feeling removed was very definitely a positive aspect of the experience: in seeking to capture footage of city life, it was important for him to be "invisible" and therefore able to video people unawares. Edward very much enjoyed the anonymity involved in being behind the camcorder, saying that in this removed position he did not have to "perform." Unlike parents who videotape family get-togethers or children's performances, he was usually videotaping people with whom he had no personal emotional relationship (although he clearly had a strong emotional attachment to the city itself).

The case of Mariya and Mikhael illustrates the contrasts between these two positions. Mariya's experience in journalism and photography led her to stress the importance of "emotional distance" when it came to getting a story or a picture. But when it came to video recordings of her daughter, she and Mikhael constructed the practice as far more intimate and private. In such moments, she felt the camcorder could be somehow "invasive": its physical presence within this private space could feel unwelcome. Mikhael said that he liked having the footage but wished the

camcorder were less obvious. While Edward wanted to be invisible himself, Mikhael wanted the *camcorder* to be invisible within these intimate
moments with his wife and daughter:

> It was just nice to film them and just to catch the atmosphere, this feeling
> between mother and daughter. On some occasions, I really do want to have
> the camera in my glasses, or it to be hidden.

In Mikhael and Mariya's case, their footage of travels around London
and Tbilisi and their accounts of this footage stand in rather stark contrast to their accounts of gathering footage involving their daughter. As
Mikhael put it:

> I didn't expect these feelings. . . . It was so nice to just film them and to catch
> the atmosphere and this feeling between mother and daughter and them doing
> something creative. They were cooking, and I didn't expect these feelings.

As we have suggested, for some video makers, being behind the camera did *not* make them feel invisible, but quite the opposite. Contrary to
the easy assumption that being behind the camera might offer a defended
hiding place from which to voyeuristically contemplate others, certain
interviewees actually spoke of this situation making them feel far *more*
self-conscious. Clearly, being the "director" (inasmuch as focusing, framing, deciding on the action to be videotaped, and so forth, can be said to
constitute direction) can make for self-consciousness. We most usually
associate feelings of self-consciousness with being the subject of the camera's gaze—with being *in front* of the camera. However, watching and
recording action through a camera lens can sometimes have the same
effect. The act of videotaping involves an invitation or insistence that
everyone present look at *me*—the camcorder lens becoming an extension of this "me." If for Edward and Neil the camcorder could make
them feel absent and invisible, for Leslie (who described her discomfort
when *using* the camcorder), Jocelyn (who described feeling "very self-
conscious" when videotaping in public), and Shanta (who avoided using
her camcorder in public because this made her feel like a "tourist") it had
the opposite effect, making them feel *too* obvious, *too* present. It is not

clear whether there is a gendered dimension here, although it is notable that it was the women in particular who expressed these feelings of self-consciousness.

Viewing action through a camcorder lens can thus entail a peculiar balance between this sense of one's own obtrusiveness and a sense of removal from the world: one is both "not there" and yet also awkwardly "there." For some, this removal was a good thing: it enabled them to avoid actually appearing on video themselves (which they imagined would have been worse), or it allowed them to capture "natural" action without having to participate in it—to remain a "fly on the wall." Yet for others, this removal was seen more negatively, as a matter of disconnecting them from participation in an emotionally important event.

In Front of the Camera

When asked about their feelings about being *in front* of the camera, participants' responses varied widely. Some, including Leslie, Nicole, Shanta, and Edward, did not enjoy being seen or seeing themselves on video. For Leslie and Nicole, however, this feeling dissipated slightly as the project went on. As Nicole explained, "I think the more you use it again, the more you get used to it, don't you? Seeing yourself and hearing yourself, so it doesn't matter as much."

Edward, however, repeated throughout the project that he did not like seeing himself on screen and pointed out that he had not even watched a professionally produced television program about ageism in which he had appeared:

> There's a trick to being in front of the camcorder. We're all actors, but some people just can't relax. . . . I feel comfortable [behind the camera]. You can't see me. They [the people being videotaped] can see me, but you [the viewer] can't. The cameraman's anonymous. See, he could be anybody. So he doesn't have to perform to the camera like they're doing. He could be standing there with Wellington boots on. It doesn't matter. So you're more comfortable. You can dress comfortable. You can pull faces. You can scratch your head. You can pick your nose . . . you're invisible.

Shanta, too, made it clear during all of our interviews that she liked being the one behind the camera doing the video making, partly because this was preferable to being in front of it:

> I like it [being behind the camera]. I like it. I don't like being *in* the recording. . . . I just don't like looking directly at a camcorder or even, you know, a picture being taken—still photos. I just don't like looking directly or posing.

Like the adults involved in the study, children varied in their reactions to appearing on screen. Aidan said of his children:

> Issy [age 3] is quite excited to see herself. . . . The boys [age 10 and 11] are usually too embarrassed. They'll film themselves and watch themselves, but they don't like other people to see it. They're self-conscious. Neither of them like performing publicly. So they feel that if someone else sees the film, it's the same thing as them performing in public.

Mariya's daughter, Alisa (age 7), also liked being videotaped and enjoyed watching her parents' reactions as they reviewed the footage. Mariya explained:

> She wants to see my reaction. But it's funny also. The reaction is one thing. Sometimes in the course of viewing she forgets my reaction completely, and she starts getting delighted. I understand that she's sort of evaluating how it is and how she is and how she could do better in future.

On the other hand, Nicole's daughter (age 10) was embarrassed and critical when watching herself on screen, as Nicole described: "And she goes, 'Oh God, didn't I look fat there?' or something. She comments on it, but she wouldn't *not* watch it." Meanwhile, Bruno's son Klaus (age 7) said that *hearing* rather than *seeing* himself on video was embarrassing: "It's embarrassing. I kind of like it [seeing himself] really, but I don't like *hearing* myself. I don't like to hear myself. Looking at myself is no problem." For Loren's son, Joe (age 11), both hearing and seeing himself on screen felt uncomfortable, which he put down to shyness: "Yeah, I don't really like hearing it. . . . I don't like being filmed. I'm just shy."

Nevertheless, much of the video data we gathered contains instances of the children openly *performing* in front of the camera: singing, larking about, dancing, videotaping themselves in front of a mirror, and so forth. While some of this was planned—as in the case of Leslie and Matt's children—other instances were much more spontaneously playful. It is undoubtedly tempting (particularly when one has never previously owned a camcorder) to see how you look, sound, and move on screen. However, we had very little evidence to suggest that adults used the camcorder in this "mirrorlike" way—with the exceptions of Loren, who began making a video diary, and Phil, who recorded himself pulling faces at the camera and also recorded little skits with his children. On the basis of our data, it would seem that both the positive and the negative aspects of appearing on screen were much more significant for the children than they were for the adults in our sample.

Watching Video

In the second part of this chapter, we move on to consider the kinds of fantasies and desires that are at stake in viewing one's video material. Before doing so, however, we need to make some observations about the immediate experience of such viewing—or its "phenomenology." Several of our participants commented on this issue, and particularly on the authenticity and veracity they associated with video. Video was generally believed to have a greater faithfulness to reality than other media, and this had particular consequences in terms of how it was watched. As Neil put it, in comparing camcorder footage with still photography:

> Kind of the difference between video and photography is that video shows the secret behind the photo, whereas the photo just shows you whatever they want you to see. It's kind of like an in-depth, behind-the-scenes look using the video.

Yaron made a similar point:

> Well, I think obviously here the still photo doesn't capture the ulterior. It doesn't capture a whole occurrence. . . . A regular still camera, it just freezes a moment in time. It doesn't sort of, have a continuity, so you don't capture a whole event.

Yaron's and Neil's claims reflect a familiar view of video as possessing a depth and complexity that still photography cannot attain: in both cases, it is seen to represent a whole or complete event but also to capture a "secret" (or an "ulterior") that takes the viewer "behind the scenes," beyond the immediate or superficial appearance of a photograph.

However, many participants talked about the marked difference between their experience of watching themselves on screen and their experiences of watching a significant other. If watching video footage of somebody close can somehow seem to "embody" them and bring them "to life," watching footage of oneself can have an almost opposite effect. It appears to alienate, almost to disembody. When we are watching someone else, video can somehow "presence" the person appearing on screen (more is said about this in the second part of this chapter), but when it comes to watching ourselves, it can make the person unfamiliar and strange. Thus, in the quotation above, Neil stressed the "in-depth, behind-the-scenes look" of video footage (referring to its "realistic" qualities) in comparison with photography, but he went on to contradict this by contrasting the videotaped (and therefore mediated) event with the "raw moment" of real life. In talking about video footage of himself playing football, he said:

> I hate seeing myself on film. I like knowing that I did it. I like the raw moment. But if I do something, like I'm on the football pitch or something, I don't like being video recorded. I like knowing that I had a raw moment of it. I know I had the moment. Everyone else who was there knows I had the moment.

For Neil, despite his stress on the realism of video (its embodiment of the "secrets" hidden by the photograph), his memories of the lived, "raw" moment are both more real and more viscerally engaging. He made this clear when talking about the different emotions evoked by watching video footage of himself playing football and by his embodied memories of this:

> Because eventually after you watch it too many times the whole feeling of achievement of what you did starts to fade a bit, because you just see it again

and again. And you just think, really and truly at the time, it felt so spectacular, but when I look back on it, it's not at all.

This sense of alienation from the real was clear from many of the participants' comments about watching themselves on video. For example, in commenting on how he felt watching footage of himself, Phil said:

> Well, disturbed. A little bit disturbed. . . . I appear to be much older than I think. It is strange. Because you kind of have an image of yourself. It was when I was twenty-seven years old or something.

Even for participants who said they liked watching their image on screen, this image was still constructed as somehow strange or unfamiliar—albeit sometimes generating a pleasant surprise. Bruno, for example, said, "I thought this was nice. Nicer than in a photo." As we have noted, for some, it was *hearing* as well as *seeing* themselves in the recorded footage that appeared "strange." Yaron, for example, commented, "I don't narrate it. I'm very self-conscious of my voice," while Leslie said, "When I hear myself talk on tape, it doesn't . . . It's not how you think it's going to be. It's very strange." Just as one's voice can feel different when heard "from the inside," so to speak, so too can one's visual image when embodied from the inside.

It is of course possible to liken people's engagement with the representation of themselves on screen with their reactions to their own image in a mirror. One might even argue that some of the participants' reactions to being videotaped could be interpreted in Lacanian terms, as constituting something very similar to the "mirror phase" of psychosexual development (Lacan 1968). According to Lacan, the infant comes to (wrongly) associate the mirror image before him or her with a sense of personal coherence or "wholeness." That image *is* him or her, somehow externalized. While a sense of satisfaction or security can attach to that sense of wholeness, so too can embarrassment and self-consciousness (although this is not something Lacan discusses). Either way, the image can have an intensely visceral effect on its "owner."

However, we do not need to resort to Lacanian language or to psychoanalysis more broadly to understand how the videotaped image can come to represent or even embody the person or place it pictures. When people watch themselves on screen, they are faced with an image that somehow "stands in" for them. However, the experience also involves a strange form of distancing, which may feel awkward or disconcerting. I look and see "me" on screen. That's me, but it's *not* me. An often uncomfortable gap lies in between the experienced, inner me and this externalized representation. For Yaron and Klaus, it is *sound* rather than *vision* that appears to produce this sense of alienation. On watching the footage, they do not recognize these voices as *theirs*. Yet for others like Neil, this also operates on a visual level.

When we watch visual footage in which we appear, what we watch is a disembodied image—an empty objectivized image of our selves. It is somehow very different from what feels like the "true," present, inner self—the present "me." The dual position of being both subject and object of the gaze entails a significant gap. This would explain why it is less difficult or unsettling to watch others on screen than it is to watch an image that is understood to represent the self. As Claparede (1911) comments, visual self-representation is a representation stripped of "all affective essence." Attempting to reconcile the present, experiencing, feeling self with that external, emptied representation on screen can create discomfort. This experienced gap or break between inner subjectivity and external representation is particularly clear when it comes to children watching video of themselves as babies. The common failure of recognition and identification is very obvious here. Children often have to be told by an adult what they are watching: the baby on screen can be unrecognizable, and some form of explanation or "anchoring" is required. As Richard Chalfen (1982) notes, the reviewing of family film or video is rarely done in complete silence. Action is narrated, people and places are identified, and meaning is talked into being.

If watching the self on screen can be somehow alienating, watching others (either present or absent) can have a radically different effect. Here the image is commonly seen to "embody" the essence of that other. It can somehow "bring to life" dead relatives, distant friends, or babies now grown. As will be illustrated in the second part of this chapter, such moving images are experienced as more than simply an emptied representation of a person. They are commonly imbued with a significance so powerful that reviewing them can make for an intensely emotional experience. Where watching oneself on screen can sometimes feel like watching something "dead" (inasmuch as its subjective essence is experienced as absent), watching another can have the almost opposite effect—of "embodying" them and so bringing them "to life." If video of another—a dead family member, a loved one living overseas or otherwise removed, a baby now grown—can somehow "presence" them into being, then footage of oneself can have an almost "absencing" effect.

Yet however "living" or present the representation of a loved other might initially feel or appear, such representations lack body. The most they can be are traces or ghosts. Both Roland Barthes (1984) and Jacques Derrida (1988), writing of photography, have referred to these "ghostly" qualities of the photograph. A significant person or place is suggested by the representation, but accompanying this suggestion is the fundamental knowledge that this person is materially absent. Video acts in a very similar way. To adapt Derrida, it can somehow "hold" or "contain" a concept—a person, place, or time. Yet the material actuality to which that concept refers can never actually or properly inhabit it. He writes:

> That concept . . . belongs to it without belonging to it; it never inscribes itself in the homogenous objectivity of framed space but instead inhabits it, or rather haunts it. (1988, 266–67)

Of photography, Barthes writes:

> If I like a photograph, if it disturbs me, I . . . look at it, I scrutinize it, as if I wanted to know more about the thing or the person it represents. . . . I want to enlarge this face in order to see it better, to understand it better, to know its truth. . . . I decompose, I enlarge . . . I *retard,* in order to have time to *know* at last. . . . Alas, however hard I look, I discover nothing: if I enlarge, I see nothing but the grain of the paper. . . . Such is the photograph: it cannot *say* what it lets us see. (1981, 99, emphasis in original)

Perhaps, then, when considering any differences between watching images of the self and images of a significant other on screen, it is more accurate to say that the former's "absence" is simply more immediately felt, because its referent is internally ever present. What the viewer knows in an immediate and intensely visceral sense is that however "present" she or he might appear within this representation, she or he is subjectively absent. The visual representation does *not* embody subjectivity. Its major characteristic is absence. By contrast, when watching significant others on screen, such a gap is primarily apparent when there is a real gap (either spatial or temporal) between the representation and the represented (e.g., the mother living abroad or the baby now grown). The represented can be seen but not touched, and this accounts for its "ghostly" quality. Representation of the self does not require this real distance for its "unreality" to be obvious. Even if footage is watched immediately, as a viewer of footage of myself, I am instantly conscious of this gap and of the fact that video, like photographic representation, does not and cannot embody my subjective essence: it looks like me, but it is *not* me. Occupying the dual position of both subject and object of the gaze therefore makes obvious the limits of representation.

PART 2: AFFECT, MEMORY, AND HISTORY

Through the making of home mode video, events and activities deemed worthy of memorialization are separated from those that are in some ways seen as "insignificant." As we discussed in the previous chapter, what is recorded is generally the familiar material of the traditional family album: children's birthday parties, family vacations and days out, and memorable public performances. Thus, one parent, Bruno, referred to his family videos as a record of "life stages." Such representations typically provide what Jo Spence (1986) and others refer to as a normative image of the "happy family" (see chapter 1). When strung together, we imagine (either consciously or unconsciously), these images will offer a happy, healthy basis for the development of identity. They will enable the maker and those appearing in the footage to somehow "return" to that moment or place and to reinhabit or reexperience the emotional experience it evoked. In doing so, they will provide a sense of security and continuity amid the ongoing experience of change and loss.

Making such records of family life is not simply common; it is constructed as an integral part of family life. As Susan Sontag (1977) put it, in writing of photography: "Not to take pictures of one's children, particularly when they are small, is a sign of parental indifference" (8). According to Sontag and others, family photography functions as a "defence against anxiety" at a time when the institution of the family is fundamentally changing (see chapter 1). As we have described, the family video makers in the study stuck closely to this established "script," producing images of family stability, success, and happiness. Only in a few instances did we see or hear about instances of conflict or upset being recorded on video. One of these instances was Neil's videos of arguments between his mother and sister—although, as we have noted, Neil argued that much of their behavior was "staged," or at least exaggerated and "played up" for the camera. In other cases we saw footage of young children who were temporarily upset over minor incidents (e.g., not getting their own way)—although these are hardly examples of any real family "dysfunction." Predictably, what we have mainly gathered is footage of "happy" or at least "functional" family stories.

As we have noted, critical commentary on this limited range of family scripts—as endlessly reproduced within photography, video, advertizing, or any number of popular media—is well established. Going *further* than a simple critique of such narratives, however, is important for understanding why they continue to be produced and the social and emotional functions they might play. Jo Spence (1995) writes, addressing family photography:

> While the media are saturated with stories of victims, unhappy families, disasters, the family records we keep for ourselves are decidedly lacking anything more than celebrations. Why is this so? The reasons are surely more profound than the fact that the advertising of companies like Kodak encourages us to have very limited types of snapshotting practices. (191–92)

Several authors have attempted an analysis of these "more profound" aspects of family photography. From Jo Spence and Patricia Holland's (1991) critical explorations of family photography, to Annette Kuhn's (1995) analysis of the myths embedded in the family photograph, to Valerie Walkerdine's (1990) examination of her own desires in relation to family photography, to Marianne Hirsch's (1997) deconstruction of the family album, the emphasis here is on issues that can be termed more "affective" or "psychosocial." These authors raise important questions about the constitution of subjectivity, fantasy, desire, and memory, and the relationship between photography and the physical embodiment of (or the failure to embody) what might be called particular "identity fictions." Rather than simply dismissing the "unrealistic" nature of such images, they attempt to understand the fantasies, fears, and desires that motivate and sustain these fictions in the first place. In the following sections, we attempt to develop some of these ideas in relation to the practice of family video making.

Fantasies of Coherence: Mapping Family Boundaries

Fantasy plays an important part in home mode video making. One feature of such fantasy to emerge from our study relates to the mapping of "family identities"—the construction of groups or communities with which one subjectively identifies. Intense emotional investments can be placed in the production and identification of a "family" through video footage. We found several instances of video being used to create and sustain links within families across generations and places. Several parents videotaped their children in order to show the footage to their own parents, who were living in distant parts of the world. Loren said that she was "devastated" when she realized that she had left her camcorder at home in London, while on a trip to Australia, where her parents live and where she herself grew up. Although the holiday was otherwise a success, it was marred by the fact that it was not videotaped. Thoughts of collecting this footage were clearly very important to Loren, and she had been telling us about this for months leading up to the trip: she had wanted the footage to bring back to the United Kingdom but also to share with her family in Australia. Similarly, Leslie sent footage of her daughters to her mother in Ireland, Yaron showed footage of his immediate family to his grandmother in Israel, and Jocelyn aimed to send a "day-in-the-life" edited video of herself and her son to her parents in Hong Kong. Shanta also described the review and circulation of her video footage among her large, extended family:

Myself, my family and their uncle's family, and their grandma, we'll watch it together and the sisters. And us and the grandma, we will sit together, which is five families. . . . And the others, like, would probably get it passed around to.

In these instances, video played an important role in keeping alive a sense of family belonging and family "identity" among a coherent group of otherwise dispersed family members. In Loren's case, for example, video footage could act as a way of "sending" her sons "home" and "bringing" her Australian family "here." In this way, we could say, the family video served to tell or remind members of their "place," to offer them a sense of emotional location that transcended geographical or physical distance.

Fantasies of Coherence: "One Day My Edit Will Come"

In the previous chapter, we looked at some of the *practical* reasons why participants did not manage to edit their footage as anticipated. However, there are clearly other, more "psychological" reasons that can be suggested for this. Deciding upon a final edit is complicated by an ever-changing present, where desires and circumstances shift. Such editing (unlike edits made for particular purposes, such as a specific person's birthday or an edit of a school play) involves the difficult decision not only of what to include but also of what to omit. As our participants commented, unless footage is divided into specific themes or subjects, home mode video remains in some ways unwatchable. As Yaron put it, "you can't replay your whole life." For him, the situation had become extreme: "we're completely saturated by recorded memories." Indeed, Bruno pointed out that at a particular school performance, half of those present in the audience had a camcorder. He appeared to find the situation quite amusing, although he himself was one of those parents. Yaron said that he learned to "get cruel" about simply getting rid of footage as a result of such experiences: "I mean, if I recorded every school play from now till they're 18, then I'd have boxes and boxes of tapes that I can never really sift through it . . . so it becomes useless."

As this implies, *omission*—or potential omission—is centrally important in the making of family video. For those (the vast majority of our participants) who had not yet tried to edit and for those who did not intend to do so, the difficult decisions touched upon here had not been faced. They were projected forward into a "one day" fantasy space where time is no issue and where decisions are clear. For example, Aidan envisaged editing the family's videos at some future moment when life might become more "organized": "Once you edit, you can organize. Otherwise, it's a mishmash. Plus, once organized it's more watchable. . . . I'll do it when I'm retired." Implicit here is the notion that the edited video story will be less chaotic than real life, with all its activity, instability, contradiction, and general "mishmash." However, Yaron was more defeatist about the possibility of achieving such coherence at some future time: "if I can't find the time *now*, why would I in ten years time?"

Clearly, if family video can be said to work in constructing particular images of a past, then it also involves fantasies of an imagined future. Virtually all the parents in our study called on this imagined time—a time when either they or their children would watch the footage, and the experience would be somehow helpful, interesting, entertaining, or otherwise valuable. Aidan, for example, suggested that the activity would be more meaningful in future that it was in the present: "Watching it now is tedious. It's more for when they're older. Maybe in 20 years' time. It'll be like a photo album."

Edward also saw the value of his footage of his grandchildren as residing not so much in the present as in the future, when it could serve as a stimulus or prompt to memory: he would be able to show the footage to their parents when they have become "horrible teenagers." Nicole, too, saw most of the value of her footage in lying the future:

> I can look back on the kids as they get older. . . . It's for when they're older, to look back on. Maybe to show their children and things. . . . In future there probably won't be many people looking through photo albums, as in a book. It will all be on the computer.

Of course these kinds of investments in the future are not limited to family video. Edward, for example, spoke about the importance and value that his footage would have in showing changes in London life.

Here he discusses the double-decker buses (the Routemasters), which are being phased out of use in the city:

> See, in years to come, people will say, "Routemaster? What's that?" . . . And I thought that while they're still running, I'd like to [videotape] as much as I can from them.

Home video footage is almost always produced for review in an imagined (historical or geographical) "elsewhere." Yet this elsewhere is always in mind at the point of production: a recording made in a specific time and place always implicates ideas of another time and place. This sense of the present speaking to the future is central to its emotional and visceral force.

Passing Time

By its very nature as a recording apparatus, the camcorder implicates time's passage. With family record keepers, however, the emotions involved in time's passage are particular. They are bound to perceptions of aging, disappearance and loss, and ultimately to mortality. Such family records testify, then, not only to *life* but also to *death*. Once grown, the baby is "gone," but not only the baby—which is an obvious example—but everyone and everything videotaped. By the time any moment is recorded, it is passed. By the time playback is under way, viewers are already watching this as a "past."

Babies are commonly videotaped much more than are older children or adults (Chalfen 1987; Rose 2003; Pini 2009). At least three reasons for this might be suggested. First, the newborn is a "novelty," and for many parents (perhaps particularly so when this is their first child) the desire to gaze at the child is very powerful. This is a significant being, expected for nine months, and until now (vague hospital scans aside) invisible as anything other than a growing bump on a mother's body. For almost a year it grows, lives, takes center stage of much conversation, planning, and thinking—and yet it is not *seen*. For most parents, the anticipation of having the baby external and "visible" is bound to be extremely strong. Often, much is already known—the baby's sex, estimated size, the color of its bedroom walls, the clothes it will wear, and frequently its name.

But it remains "invisible." Arguably, where video is concerned, the camcorder lens behaves, once the baby is born, as an extension of this intense gaze, with its accompanying feelings of anticipation, curiosity, anxiety, and love.

Second, newborns, toddlers, and young children change their appearance very quickly compared to adults. They are very rapidly developing into something different. As much as they change visually, they can be seen to "disappear." As many of the participants in our project described, the desire to "capture" or freeze is more intense precisely because of such movement. Before their eyes, their babies are quickly becoming "not babies." They are constantly "disappearing." By contrast, older children and adult family—whose visual appearance does not alter as significantly—do not appear to be surrounded by this sense of fast-approaching loss. As Leslie commented, "They're kids, and it's over in a flash, you know. Even from, you know, a year ago, they've changed."

The third reason why babies might be videotaped more than adults and older children relates to what we might describe as the "narrative" aspects of video. In many ways, the production and interpretation of video are bound to be related to our typical expectations of conventional realist narrative film, where everything leads somewhere and there is a linear progression toward an end point. Babies in this respect signify the beginning of a life story. When watching such footage, the viewer knows something that the video maker at the time did not know: what happens next. This hindsight aspect of watching home mode video changes its meaning. The viewer knows more than the image in itself can ever contain. Again, some kind of "gap" is central to the subjective experience of video making. What is missing or absent from the footage is the reviewing present—which is entirely fundamental to its meaning.

There is a sense with family video that a linear tale is being told—a story of a life "unfolding." In order to tell this life story, different fragments of evidence are collected of its stages. Signs of more rapid change make more obvious time's passage, which is ultimately the movement toward death. Indeed, Richard Chalfen (1987) refers to the "freezing time" aspect of family video as the "defeating death" motivation behind its production. He notes the observed tendency for people to photograph more during times of rapid change and argues, "By increasing the frequency of picture-taking during times of change, people could be said to be slowing down the inevitable process of change and development" (134).

Participants involved in our study supported Chalfen's observation. Many reported videotaping first-born children more than others and gradually videotaping less as children grow. Aidan, for example, described how his eldest son, Max, was filmed more often as a baby and more often than his subsequent children: "My father-in-law filmed Max a lot but then lost interest. Yeah, the first one got filmed a lot."

Videotaping is about visually recording a "present," which is imagined (while being recorded) as a "past" when reviewed in an imagined "future" (even if this is only a very near future, as when families watch their video of a day's outing when the family gets home). Awareness that this practice is about turning the present into a "memory" is therefore always apparent. The moment that the camcorder "record" button is pressed, somewhere within the experience of video making lie images of the "future" and the making of the "past." Annette Kuhn (1995) argues:

> Remembering is clearly an activity that takes place for, as much as in, the present. Is memory then not understood better as a position or a point of view in the current moment than as an archive or a repository of bygones? Perhaps memory offers a constantly changing perspective on the places and times through which we—individually and collectively—have been journeying? Perhaps it is only when we look back that we make a certain kind of sense of what we see? (128)

Likewise, Marianne Hirsch (2003) writes of family photography, "Photography interrupts, actually stops time, freezes a moment, and is inherently elegiac" (72).

Although Hirsch is referring specifically to still photography, this notion of retaining present moments on video for future "elegaic" contemplation was a key motivation for many of our participants. Video, in that it entails *moving* images, is perhaps more aptly spoken of in terms of "capturing" rather than freezing—which implies stability and immobility. Nevertheless, as with still photography, there is a sense that through reviewing footage the viewer can somehow reembody that place and time and reexperience the emotions involved. Like many of our participants, Mariya spoke of her desire for such a return or reexperiencing:

> I just miss the past. So every time, you know, the moment is gone. So my idea of photographs and video is sort of freezing the moments, the pleasure of life. I am really enjoying life. And one day if it's not there. . . . And I want my daughter to see how things are and were. . . . I think she will really appreciate it when she grows up to see what life was like now. So I am trying to get . . . capture what I feel about life, what to me life is. The beauty of it and the beauty of places and simple things. So I am really excited. I'm taking it [the camcorder] around with me anywhere, any time really.

Although Mariya clearly knows that video cannot take the viewer *back*, watching the footage can activate intense emotions that are associated with what is being viewed—emotions that may be far more intense than (and are certainly always different from) any that may have actually been experienced at the time.

While family video making can obviously be likened to family photography, there are some fundamental differences. With photographs stored in a family album, a sense of movement and continuity making up the life story comes through only by turning pages and gazing at static images. Although these may well be ordered in a way that demonstrates a sequence of "life stages," there is no material movement involved. With video, the story appears to flow and unravel of its own accord. Unlike the still photograph, it contains the passage of time in itself: it is *real* time that the viewer is sitting through. There is a very important difference between still photography and video in this respect. As Barthes (1984) asserts in relation to photography, that which is pictured *did* exist in the real world: "Photography never lies; or rather, it can lie as to the meaning of the thing, being by nature tendentious, never to its existence" (87).

Video also embodies this "having been there" quality, but it offers more, because the act of watching also involves the passing of time. The viewer's present passing of time, as he or she sits and watches, identically mirrors the passage of time for those on screen. Even within edited footage, action in specific clips is "action in time." So although a desire to somehow freeze time for the purposes of revisiting it in the future is apparent in all of our participants' accounts, the situation is more about capturing events *as they move through time*. And on watching the footage, as the action is taken forward, so is the viewer. This is part of video's visceral pull: it takes *you* with it.

VIDEO MAKING, EXPERIENCE, AND EMOTION: A CONCLUSION

This chapter has explored some of the emotional dimensions of video making—in terms of both the immediate experience itself and its functions in sustaining memory and identity. These emotions are temporally and spatially situated and are therefore necessarily different, necessarily specific to the context. Yet they arise both from the present context and from an imagined future context, in which they will necessarily be different.

Video cannot simply take one back to a past emotion, just as it cannot "bring to life" something or someone absent. Reviewing can activate new emotions, but these are inevitably different from any emotions that may have been experienced at the time of recording, because the "present" while watching footage is different from the "present" during recording. As such, video does not take the viewer back into a past emotional state—this would be impossible. As Claparede (1911) argues:

> It is impossible to feel emotion as past. . . . One cannot be a spectator of one's own feelings: one feels them or one does not feel them. One cannot imagine them without stripping them of their affective essence. . . . My past self is psychologically distinct from my present self . . . it is an empty objectivised self, which I continue to feel at a distance from my true self which lives in the present. (367–69)

Jill Bennett (2005) remarks, in reference to Claparede's statement, that emotions are felt as they are experienced: as remembered events, they become representations. The conceptual work implied in the act of remembering—of representing to oneself—entails a kind of distanced perception: one *thinks* rather than simply *feels* the emotion.

Nevertheless, video can bring into presence a powerful suggestion or trace of a person or a time that is now past and perhaps lost forever. This suggestion can have a powerful affective and visceral impact. In the meeting of a "ghostly" yet nevertheless powerful "trace" with the equally powerful knowledge of this material absence, the space is opened for the workings of fantasy. Indeed, the entire practice is largely meaningless without fantasy and imagination. The future cannot be felt, and the past cannot be revisited in an identical form. We know that the now-grown baby cannot be held, and the child viewing footage of its family overseas cannot experience, in an embodied sense, belonging within that family. Yet none of these things necessarily makes the emotional impact of such video making any less real.

CHAPTER 5

Learning Video:
The Making of Media Literacy

In this chapter, our analysis focuses on the issue of media literacy. Media literacy in its various forms—visual literacy, television literacy, cine-literacy, and so on—has been a focus of discussion for several decades, yet it has recently become an important theme both in cultural policy and in wider public debate. In an age of proliferating media sources and outlets, and of more participatory media, media literacy has come to be seen as a kind of alternative to centralized regulation or at least as a key dimension of a modernized regulatory strategy. Others have argued, more broadly, that a competent and well-informed understanding of the media is a prerequisite of contemporary citizenship.

There have been many debates about how to define media literacy and about the value of the analogy with print literacy. We do not intend to explore these in detail here. On a basic "functional" level, media literacy involves the ability to *access* media for particular purposes. Just as print literacy entails the ability to decode and encode written language (e.g., to turn letters into sounds), so media literacy entails a basic competence in locating, using, and interpreting media. Yet when we talk about somebody being a "literate" person, we generally mean that they can do more than simply read and write. The term *literacy* also implies broader forms of cultural or critical understanding.

For our purposes here, the term *media literacy* refers primarily to one's understanding of the "language" of a given medium—which obviously includes the audiovisual "languages" of image and sound. This implies a recognition that media representations are deliberately constructed and that they inevitably present selective or partial views of the world. Beyond that, media literacy is often seen to entail an informed understanding of the technological, economic, and political processes that determine how media are produced, circulated, and consumed. These kinds of insights are typically represented in media education syllabuses and curriculum documents as a set of "key concepts" (see Buckingham 2003).

However, it is important to recognize that media literacy is not simply a matter of critical study and analysis. Media educators typically argue that the key conceptual understandings that make up media literacy can be developed effectively—and often in more engaging ways—through the experience of media production. Likewise, the UK media regulator Ofcom defines media literacy not simply in terms of the ability to access, use, and understand media, but also in terms of the ability to *create* media texts and to use media in order to communicate (Ofcom 2004).

Developing this creative ability is by no means simply a matter of spontaneous "self-expression" or of technical skill. As with any other medium or art form, making videos that are meaningful to others does not depend merely on the ability to operate particular items of equipment or to use specific software applications. It is also about understanding the "language" or grammar of the medium—for example, making informed choices about the composition and framing of shots and about camera movements; ordering or editing shots into narratives or sequences that make coherent sense; and deploying semiotic resources such as sound and music, gesture and movement, and even lighting and special effects, to achieve particular purposes. Effective communication also means thinking about one's target audience—how to engage them, direct their attention, and encourage them to "read" in particular ways.

One of the key issues for educators in this field is the relationship between consumption and production. To what extent does people's experience as "consumers" (readers or users) of media inform how they produce? And how might the experience of production impact back on consumption, enabling us to interpret media in a more informed or perhaps critical way? It could be argued that ordinary consumers have an extensive latent (or "passive") knowledge about media, which can somehow be activated by the experience of media production—just as language learning entails transforming the extensive knowledge we gain as listeners and readers into "active" knowledge that we can use as speakers or writers.

Much of the discussion of media literacy relates to formal educational settings such as schools. Yet clearly people may acquire media literacy through their everyday encounters with media, not only as consumers but also as producers. Media may effectively "teach" the competencies that people need in order to use and interpret them, and the everyday experience of making media—for example, in the form of snapshot photography or home video—may also require and develop forms of media literacy. Yet in the informal setting of the home or the peer group, people are generally less likely to learn in systematic or structured ways; it may not be necessary for them to make their "latent" knowledge explicit or to reflect upon what they do, and there may be little requirement to create "finished products" that can be shared or circulated more widely. Creative activity in such settings may be less a matter of sustained application and self-discipline—of the kind that Robert Stebbins (2007) sees as characteristic of "serious leisure"—and more to do with casual play and experimentation, with tinkering or messing about, and with very occasional and uncommitted engagement.

Yet this is not to say that such informal uses are insignificant in themselves. Indeed, we would argue that they can play a vital role in developing people's media literacy. In the second part of this chapter, we explore *what* people learn about media from their experience as home video makers. We look at their knowledge of the "language" of film and video, their use of the media forms and genres they are familiar with from their everyday consumption of media, their understanding of the potential or "affordances" of video as a medium, and their sense of an audience for their productions. Yet this discussion begs some prior questions. To what extent are such issues actually important to people in the first place? What kinds of knowledge or skill do they feel are necessary for them to acquire? Why, in short, would they be bothered to become "media literate"?

Exploring these issues thus raises some fundamental questions about *how* and *why* these understandings might be acquired and developed, particularly in the informal setting of the home. What motivates people to want to learn about media, to deepen their understanding, or to make it more systematic? In addressing these questions, which we do in the first part of this chapter, we will need to account for learning as a social process that occurs through interaction and dialogue and as a highly contingent, contextual phenomenon. In doing so, we will draw on theories of learning that regard it as a matter of social activity and participation, rather than as a merely internal, psychological matter.

As we have seen, there were some significant differences across our 12 households in terms of people's domestic circumstances, social positions, and individual motivations. While some of our participants remained with the home mode, using their cameras to record everyday family life and special family occasions, others sought to orientate their work toward a more public setting—even if this ambition was rarely achieved. In many (and various) ways, this often involved creating videos that related more directly to existing media forms or genres, that might serve (either now or in the future) as a more public record, or that might be used to communicate with a wider audience.

These differences of context and purpose are also reflected in the forms of media literacy that were acquired here. Several of our participants expressed the wish to develop their skills in using media, in terms not merely of their mastery of the technology but also of the language of the medium. However, not all of them had sufficient time or energy or motivation to do so, and some clearly saw this more systematic kind of learning as unnecessary or superfluous, given that their ambitions were relatively limited. As such, we would argue against a normative or singular view of media literacy, as a fixed set of skills and understandings that people should somehow be expected or required to possess. Rather, we would suggest that there are multiple literacies, which reflect people's different social circumstances and motivations.

PART I: LEARNING

In analyzing and comparing the different ways in which our participants learned about video making, we considered a series of subsidiary questions. These were, first, about *planning*. To what extent was video making merely a spontaneous activity, or was it more self-conscious and reflexive? How far did our participants plan what they were going to do prior to filming or engage in editing or other "postproduction" activities? *Moti-*

vation is our second major theme here. What motivated participants to want to learn how to make "better" videos? To what extent, and in what ways, did they evaluate their video making, and what criteria did they use? Our third theme is to do with the *methods* that the participants used in order to learn. To what extent did they rely on the camcorder manual, on trying to copy what they had seen, or on other people's advice—or did they learn primarily through "trial and error"? Finally, we look more broadly at the participants' own *reflections* on the learning process. To what extent, and in what ways, did they define themselves as "learners" in the first place? How did they conceptualize the learning process? And how did this relate to the kind of identity they took on as video makers and the role video making played in their lives?

The Best-Laid Plans . . .

Beyond generally deciding to take the camera along, or get it out, on particular occasions, there was little sense that our participants engaged in much advance planning. Video making was typically seen as a spontaneous activity, rather than something that should be prepared or planned ahead of time. For most, it was a matter of "just recording moments" (as Loren put it). Indeed, some argued that it was precisely this spontaneity that was most important; as we have seen in chapter 3, the disadvantage of the camcorder, as opposed to the still camera or (in particular) the mobile phone, was that it wasn't always conveniently at hand. Participants had to remember to pack it, and it was rather bulky, and this required a degree of planning that several participants found hard to incorporate in their busy everyday lives.

Even so, there were some interesting exceptions to this spontaneous approach and some instances where video making clearly involved significant planning and preparation. This was most apparent for participants who sought alternatives to the private home mode. For example, Phil's "rubbish chute" video meant remembering to record himself as he took out the trash every day—something that he described as involving "discipline," and it also involved some experimentation to find the correct angle and location "so it would look good, and where you could see what was going on." Jocelyn also planned ahead for the travelogue she shot in Paris:

I was thinking ahead as to what sorts of shots I wanted, as well as random just filming everything. Things like the shots in the cathedral with the stained glass. . . . I took a few different frames of that. . . . Taking things at different angles and then just choosing the right sort of set-ups. So that was where I was really thinking, "Okay, I need little drop-ins, to break up—to give the flavor of Paris."

Aidan and Ted's family also had to engage in some quite elaborate advance planning for Ted's spoofs, which involved specific locations and special effects. Ted's remake of *Lost* was partly shot on a family outing to Kew Gardens, where some convincingly tropical foliage could be found, while his version of *Jaws* made good use of a trip to the London Aquarium. The sequence of his father, Aidan, being attacked by the shark was videotaped in very cold seawater in France, with the camera contained in a plastic bag (which proved to be a costly mistake!). Even so, Aidan's attempts to encourage Ted to produce a script or to "map it out a bit beforehand" were largely in vain: much of what took place was "made up on the spot," with other family members being summarily directed into position.

Advance planning also played a role for the more systematic home mode video makers. Yaron's contribution to the wedding video—described in chapter 3—involved a considerable amount of rehearsal, and some scenes were shot several times as the children gradually refined their performances. Matt and Leslie's children also prepared short skits and performances for the camera, although they were not particularly interested in watching them, which would suggest that in this case the act of performance itself was more important than the video. Phil also said he was most interested in instances where the children were "performing for the camera"—although as we shall see, there was some ambivalence here about the need to capture more "natural" behavior. Even Shanta, one of the most home mode–oriented of our participants, described how she tried to capture some "atmosphere" of the school before going on to record her own children's participation in an assembly performance.

Nevertheless, these examples remain exceptional. Most of what our participants did with their camcorders was not prepared, planned, or orchestrated in advance. Even for those who sought to create more elaborate productions, this was not their typical practice. Many of our participants had more adventurous ideas that they had not managed to see through—and as we have seen in chapter 3, there were various reasons for this. Yet in reality, spontaneous, even haphazard use was very much the norm.

Wise after the Event

Similar points apply to editing and other "postproduction" activities. Although we went to great lengths to ensure that all our participants had the possibility of editing (only Edward, who did not have a computer at home, would have had to do this at the community center), very few of them took the opportunity to do so. Many expressed the intention to learn to edit at some point in the future, at least when we asked them, but there were hardly any examples throughout the year of any of our participants producing anything that they themselves regarded as a "finished production." We heard some reports of editing—Neil told us that his brother had recorded himself emceeing and posted the results on MySpace, while Ted apparently edited some of his spoof material with the help of his father—but we saw hardly any actual evidence of this. The tapes we gathered and analyzed were almost entirely comprised of unedited "raw" footage.

Such material was often painfully boring for us to watch—not so much because of its technical limitations as because of its lack of personal or emotional significance for us. However, we did not get a strong sense that our participants spent a great deal of time watching it either. Matt and Leslie, who were relatively systematic home mode video makers, described how they would watch their footage when they got back home from a family outing; while Matt also reviewed the material in the course of transferring it to DVD so he could send it to his mother. For Matt, editing was essentially a matter of "tidying up" as he copied from one format to another and did not involve the use of editing software: he aimed to "keep the interesting bits and leave everything else out" and estimated that he copied about 80 percent of what he had videotaped. Yet even he described how they and their children would "get bored of watching it"—in contrast with their collection of family photographs, which they were still keen to look through on a regular basis.

Like most of our participants, Nicole recognized that her footage would need editing if it was to become "watchable," although she admitted that she would probably only have an incentive to edit when she had finally used up all the tapes we had provided. In fact, Nicole had experimented with editing but realized that she would have to have a purpose if she was going to learn more about it. Ultimately, though, she doubted whether she would be any more likely to watch edited material: "I don't know how much you would watch, you know, and how many times over you'd watch it." Similar points were made by Yaron, who was one of the few participants to edit. He felt that he didn't view even his edited videos enough to warrant the amount of time he had spent on them:

> That's probably the reason why we've sort of stopped taking film. Because this holiday, I shot an hour or so of footage, I spent then the few hours I needed to do the editing, then uploading and all that, and we've watched it two or three times, close after I did it, and never since.

As we saw in chapter 3, the reluctance or failure to edit was partly a technical issue and partly a matter of skills. Several participants noted that video took up considerable amounts of storage space on their computer; and Bruno also argued that copying to the hard disk would result in a loss of quality, saying that he preferred to keep tapes. Some may have been daunted by the potential complexity of the software, although in fact relatively few ever reached that stage. The central issue was one of motivation: very few of the participants had much reason to want to learn about editing or to create "finished productions." When specifically asked, most expressed the wish to edit, if only to keep all their best material together on one tape. However, for most this was simply a matter of good intentions, rather than an activity they were able or inclined to prioritize right now—although (as we have noted) Aidan ironically suggested that he might get around to it when he retired.

Even those who already had some editing skills, or might easily have developed them, did very little in practice. Loren's older son, Barney, had learned about video editing as part of a special project in his English lessons at school, and he also recognized that there would be a purpose in editing his homemade material:

There's not much point in recording if I'm not going to edit, because it's just a bunch of footage mixed up. . . . If it's not edited I just feel like I can't watch it, because it's not done properly so that you can watch it all in one go.

Barney expected that his involvement in gathering material for a Duke of Edinburgh award (which recognizes young people's involvement in hobbies, sports, and volunteering) might provide some additional incentive. But like his mother, he had an almost fatalistic sense that he was never going to "get around" to editing. Even Edward, by far the most prolific of our participants, failed to explore editing. In his case, this is something he would have had to arrange at the local community center—although he had made use of its facilities to pursue his photography. Edward described how he wanted to create title cards for his videos "to make it look posh," but in general he claimed to make a virtue of trying to edit in camera. Editing, he argued, was a matter of "cutting lumps out"—and "if you need to edit, you shouldn't have took it" (i.e., videotaped it in the first place).

As we have seen, Jocelyn was the only one of our participants to engage in significant amounts of editing. She had observed editors at work while employed at an advertising agency; and, as we have described, she had some ambitions to become a scriptwriter herself. Video making thus served a role in terms of developing her understanding of the medium or "learning the technique"—"and that also shows me how difficult it is to actually put something brilliant together—which helps me understand in terms of writing for someone else to film and putting it together, how to put it all in place." Even so, Jocelyn drew a fairly clear line between her screen writing ambitions and her video making, which did not go far beyond the private home mode: her aim in editing was essentially to cut out what she called the "random filming" in order to create shorter and more coherent videos to send to her parents in Australia. She admitted that she had found the process "tiresome" and had quite quickly come up against the limitations of the basic editing software she was using. She described these productions—of which she had made one, the video of her trip to Paris, with another in progress—as "little films . . . just little postcards." As we shall see, this sense of a concrete, known audience for one's productions provides a key motivation for learning.

However, the fantasy of a future point at which they would review and edit their tapes was important for many of our participants. As we saw in chapter 4, many of them were gathering video not so much for present viewing but for posterity, as a means of prompting memories in the future. They projected forward to a time in which the material they were filming would seem somehow much more poignant and meaningful than it did right now. By contrast, reviewing it now seemed almost beside the point. Indeed, even if the fantasy of editing was never achieved, the knowledge that the material was available—that one's memories were somehow contained on a tape or in a computer file that could be accessed at any time—seemed to offer a sense of "ontological security" in an ever-changing world.

Doing It by the Book?

How did our participants learn about video making? Mariya, who is from the former Soviet republic of Georgia, provided a theory about cultural differences in this respect in an e-mail she sent us:

> Different nations seem to have different learning cultures, that proves to be true for simple cases, such as camcorder use. From my observation, it's become a custom, a culture, call it what you will, in the UK and other developed West to learn things by manuals, i.e., reading first. In the developed and equally educated East, however, still, learning by doing seems to be common. I learned by trial and error and by asking more experienced users what they do and how. I'd love to have a little recording (included with the camera itself) to tell me what to do and what are the possibilities of the camera when I first pick it up, as I find it boring to put aside the sexy gadget when you unpack it and start reading a manual.

Mariya claimed to have found support for her theory with a sample of eight of her Georgian and British friends. Although our own sample is only a little larger, and is certainly ethnically diverse, it does not support her assertions. Hardly any of our participants, not even the most dedicated and prolific video makers, claimed to have read the manual at all closely. In fact, Mariya's partner, Mikhael (who is also from Georgia), was one of the few to consult the manual, along with seeking expert advice online. Many shared Mariya's wish to have a single source of important information; but in no case did the manual seem to serve that function.

Like Mikhael, some of the more technologically proficient of our participants did seem to have consulted the manual at some stage, although all said that they preferred to use on-screen menus or straightforward trial and error. All of these manual readers were men, while women seemed to be more likely to ignore the manual entirely and confine themselves to the most basic controls—which might suggest that there is a gender dimension in play here (or at least that participants were making implicit claims about gender). Yet in all cases, the manual seemed to be a source of last resort—"if all else fails," as Leslie put it. Even Edward, the most prolific of our participants, claimed that he read the manual only after a period of use and experimentation. Matt was typical in claiming that he consulted the manual only "vaguely" and "for the basics," but that he generally preferred trial and error.

This may partly have reflected a general view of the camcorder as a fairly straightforward device and a sense that there was not much to learn anyway. Loren and Barney, for example, said that the camera itself was "straightforward . . . press the button and record," while Edward described it as "idiot proof." However, it also reflected a shared preference for learning through discovery. There were several instances here of participants coming across quite complex possibilities almost by accident, simply through "messing about" or trying out options on the on-screen menus. Thus, Neil discovered that it was possible to select a more directional microphone that would cut out background noise. Matt found a backlight control that was helpful when shooting indoors against a window, while Loren worked out how to do autofades, an effect she preferred to straight cuts. In other cases, interesting techniques could be acquired by accident: Edward discovered some pleasing effects when shooting city lights at night, while Matt achieved what he called "psychedelic" effects by using the backlight control. In many instances, the participants had not sought to achieve these effects or known they were possible. They were simply playing with the camera, or as Neil put it, "I just kept pressing through the menu, to see what happens."

When it came to editing, trial and error was also the predominant approach. As we have noted, Jocelyn had seen professionals editing but nevertheless tried to figure out the software for herself—and was then frustrated to discover that it cut up her footage automatically into sections of a fixed length and would not allow her to import her own music tracks. Aidan was been annoyed by the tendency of simple editing programs to "prepackage" the material. In his case, however, he took a relatively pedagogical approach to encouraging his son Ted's movie-making adventures. While there were certainly important elements of trial and error and of playful experimentation here, Aidan was also attempting to teach Ted about the "techniques" of video making and the role of editing:

> He originally thought you filmed it all in order. And you say, no, we can take this bit and stick it there, film whatever bits you want in whatever order. You know, be down at the seaside, and you can do all the bits that involve being in the water there.

Likewise, in helping his 10-year-old son Ted create a homage to a Nike ad, Aidan showed him how clever footballing tricks could be "faked" by means of clever editing, as in the case of the film *Bend It like Beckham:*

> I was trying to explain to them . . . when you see a movie, what you'll see is somebody kick the ball, then you'll see the ball flying into the net. You don't see the whole thing continuously. So I'll say, "Watch. I'll film you shooting. Now I'll have the film in the camera. Now you throw the ball into the top corner of the net. Now look how it goes, it looks like you shot and it went into the corner."

In this relatively formal teaching, it was also notable that Aidan and Ted moved back and forth between experimentation and using the manual, for example, in attempting to achieve the "subaquatic effects" Ted wanted for his *Jaws* remake. Aidan reinforced this process by drawing Ted's attention to tricks and effects achieved in mainstream media, an issue to which we shall return below.

Learning from Your Mistakes

Although all our participants were broadly positive about owning the camcorder and exploring its possibilities, their initial experiences were often characterized by disappointment. This may partly have been because they felt obliged to meet our expectations as researchers—although we repeatedly insisted that whatever they did (or did not do) was absolutely fine with us. Yet the participants were frequently apologetic about the quality and the amount that they had videotaped: Jocelyn, who probably had higher expectations than most, described her early efforts as "really bad," "silly," and "stupid," and she was not alone in this respect. As we have noted above, there was only limited evidence of participants actually watching their footage more than once, let alone any indication of careful or rigorous evaluation. Nevertheless, there were several instances in which they clearly had learned from their own mistakes.

Some of these mistakes were essentially "technical." Some were relatively basic, such as accidentally erasing material or zooming in the wrong direction. Shanta, Nicole, and Yaron were among several who described how they had been disappointed by their shaky camera work and tried to avoid this on subsequent occasions. Bruno managed to discover an automatic antishake device using the in-screen menu and eventually invested in a tripod, while Neil learned to rest the camera on his knee while videotaping football and to use two hands rather than one. Several participants learned that zooming in close would accentuate the unsteadiness of the image, while others discovered that too much zooming in and out—particularly at full speed—was likely to make for queasy viewing.

Other aspects were more to do with aesthetic effects. Jocelyn, for example, was particularly concerned about the quality of lighting and the overall "look" of the video. She also described how she had discovered the importance of the direct gaze while video blogging:

It's like talking to yourself in the mirror. But when you're actually looking at it, it's more interesting to have the eye contact with the lens for that sort of stuff. So, sort of picking back as I watch things that I've filmed, I thought,

"Oh yeah, I'd do that a bit differently, I'd change that." So it's all a learning curve.

Yet in most instances, the concern was primarily with content—and especially with the need to be more selective. As Bruno put it, one surprising thing that the novice video maker quickly learns is "how quickly something gets boring." Thus, Mikhael described how viewing his initial attempts led him to think in terms of "shorter bits"—"the most important parts of the action—two or three parts, it will be enough." Like several other participants, he was effectively learning to "edit in camera." Similarly, Nicole described a video she had recorded of a family visit to a farm:

> When you play it back and watch, you know what not to do the next time you do it. . . . I mean, I think we filmed for about 20 minutes of the whole day of going to the farm, and that was enough . . . You could keep stopping and starting, like you would if you were taking a picture.

Matt likewise described how reviewing his material while transferring it onto DVD was teaching him to be more selective in future: rather than simply videotaping the children "running around in circles or whatever," he was filming more prepared scenes. Matt also saw this as a consequence of the novelty of the camcorder beginning to wear off, a phenomenon that other participants described as well.

Nevertheless, for more committed video makers like Edward, Jocelyn, and Ted, this was a more systematic, ongoing project: each experience would lead to reflection, which would then feed into the next attempt. For Edward, this was an approach he had developed in his previous work as an amateur photographer, and it was sometimes accompanied by a closer reading of the manual:

> If I can go back to when I got a first camera, which I think was a Box Brownie [laughs] . . . I just like go out and take pictures with it and see what mistakes I made, and then I read the instruction book, and it makes more sense. If I tried to read the instruction book first, I'm lost, but when I've made the

mistakes, that will be an experience, and when I read the instruction book, it makes sense.

Similarly, Aidan described how his son Ted would review his footage in the camera viewfinder: "He'll sort of wind it back and say, 'Oh, that's a good shot,' or he didn't get it properly, so he wants to go back and do it again. . . . He's hypercritical." In such instances, we can observe a relatively systematic process of trial and error, which is driven partly by a formal or artistic sense of what makes for a "good shot." Even so, this was relatively unusual among our participants: for most, avoiding mistakes was essentially about capturing content more effectively and economically, rather than pursuing any more ambitious creative agenda.

Learning Identities

As we saw in chapter 3, the participants in our study had different images of themselves as video makers and different perceptions of the role of video making in their lives. These differences were also reflected in their different styles and methods of learning. Some came to regard video making as a hobby or a project in its own right and hence as something they needed to work at in order to improve their technique. For others, it was merely a casual part of everyday life: it was not something that needed or deserved concentrated attention—and even if they had wanted to give it such attention, many found that they were practically unable to do so.

A key aspect of this was obviously the participants' broader orientations toward the family—both nuclear and extended. Documenting and even celebrating the family remains the overriding motivation for very many amateur video makers—although, as we argued in chapter 4, this process is often more complex and ambivalent than some critics have tended to suggest. The more "family oriented" of our participants thus had a particular motivation to learn. These were predominantly, though by no means exclusively, women—and in some contexts, this seemed to cut across a tendency for men to be seen as the controllers of technology within the family (a tendency that has been well documented in media research; see, e.g., Morley 1986, Gray 1992, and many others). As a result, the "gendering" of home video making was by no means straightforward: for example, Shanta, Nicole, and Mariya, rather than their husbands, did most of the videotaping, although Bruno, Phil, Yaron, and Matt tended to take the leading role in their families—and in many of these cases, video making provided a means for these men to express and share their love for, and pride in, their children.

On the other hand, some of our participants derived their identity as video makers from their role as workers—either currently or as former or aspiring future workers—or from previous "serious leisure" interests. This was most evidently the case with Edward's identity as a former bus driver and as a keen amateur (and indeed semiprofessional) photographer, but it was also reflected to a lesser extent in Yaron's and Mikhael's professional involvement with digital technology and in Jocelyn's career aspirations. Thus, Edward declared himself to be more than a mere "hobbyist": "I'd love to do it professionally. I would say that I'm seriously interested in this." As such, he was quite self-conscious about learning technique and sought to attain the kind of fluency he had managed to achieve with his still photography: "If you use a still camera, you don't think of it anymore, you just do it. . . . It's like walking down the street, you don't think about putting a leg in front of the other." As an academic scientist, Bruno was particularly interested in the technical aspects of video making and expressed the wish to become more "systematic" in his approach. Meanwhile, as a semiprofessional musician and performer, Phil had shot some material for a promotional video and wished to improve his technique in areas such as framing and lighting. Barney had taken a photography course at school and was interested in further study in this area; he too was setting out to "learn more skills" in a more or less systematic way—"I kind of made a competition for myself to be good by the end of the year."

In some instances, this was part of a pedagogic relationship between parent and child. As we have seen, this was particularly apparent with Aidan and his son Ted. Aidan responded very enthusiastically to his son's interest in video making and clearly saw him as having a spontaneous creative ability in this area. While Aidan himself was interested in the area—and had a cousin who was a keen amateur video maker—he also set out to teach his son specific video making techniques. Jocelyn also projected some of her own creative ambitions on to her son Jack: she was keen on Jack using video for "expressing himself," writing stories and "bringing them to life" with video, although she said that she did not want him to "get into that industry."

Participants who were moving beyond the private form of the home mode, and seeking (however hypothetically) to locate their work within a more public context, were thus more likely to see themselves as engaged in a more systematic and disciplined process of learning. As we have seen, Jocelyn discussed her use of video in terms of a "learning curve," describing herself as a mere "novice" who had so far only "scratched the surface." She claimed that she did not use the camera spontaneously or "carry it around on spec," but rather used it for "specific projects." Even so, there was often a gap between aspiration and reality here. Yaron, for example, recognized that becoming an accomplished filmmaker required a great deal of work—more work (in his view) than with other media such as still photography, not least because of the complexity of the technology. He noted that his children would fantasize about making videos, but compared with the quick results they could obtain from drawing or painting, making a video took much longer. This in itself acted as a deterrent: "Maybe by now they realize that if you want to get quality, you need to work very hard about it, and they don't really expect to be able to produce that quality, so they don't even bother." Mariya also saw herself as a creative artist—or potential artist—who was interested in alternatives to the home mode. She spoke about wanting to make a "beautiful film" and about "capturing emotions" and "the beauty of personal relations"—although in practice most of her footage is fairly indistinguishable from that of other participants with much less grandiose ambitions.

By contrast, for many of our participants, the home mode was the limit of their ambitions. Shanta, for example, did not want to "walk around and record for the sake of it": she was simply interested in videotaping her children. Even so, her family trip to Bangladesh did result in some more sustained and even "artistic" attempts at video making—and it was notable that it was only at this stage that her husband became involved. Likewise, for Nicole (as we shall see in more detail below), there was a sense that attention to the more technical or artistic aspects of video making was unnecessary for what she wanted to do. The same was true for Leslie and Matt: while Matt was interested in using technology in relation to making his own music, when it came to video he was not looking to go beyond the private home mode. Like several other participants, he simply wanted to make "watchable" home videos—and in the process, sought to become more discerning and selective: yet here again, the key emphasis was on content, rather than on stylistic or technical issues.

An Interim Conclusion: Informal, Situated Learning

To sum up, we can say that for most of our participants, most of the time, video making was not a focused activity that they engaged in for its own sake. It was merely a secondary dimension of other activities and relationships—something added, certainly, but not something indispensable. However, there were exceptions to this. Some of our participants did develop an interest in the activity in its own right. While some were unable to follow through on this, or just not sufficiently motivated to do so, we suspect that for a few at least, it might eventually become a more sustained interest.

Yet even for these potentially dedicated few, learning was primarily achieved by doing, by trial and error. It was not especially self-conscious, systematic, or deliberate. It was not an "academic" process, and it did not involve much theoretical speculation. In this respect, it can be seen to exemplify the "informal" styles of learning that have generated increasing interest among educational researchers in recent years (e.g., Coffield 2000; Sefton-Green 2004). Informal learning does not involve explicit teaching, or participation in educational institutions, or indeed any external assessment. It is typically integrated within the routine activities of everyday life, rather than being perceived as somehow separate and in need of special attention. It is essentially self-motivated and attuned to the needs and purposes of the individual—although that is not to say that it is necessarily the most efficient or effective way to learn.

Even so, for all our participants, learning also involved a degree of reflection, of looking back at what they had done and trying to understand how it might be improved—and while this reflection was primarily focused on the need to capture content, it also addressed questions of aesthetics and technique. While it may have been "informal," this learning was not entirely lacking in discipline, self-evaluation, and the desire to progress.

Looking back to the continuum we introduced in chapter 3, we can broadly say that the more public forms of amateur video making are associated with a more elaborated form of media literacy and with a more deliberate and reflexive approach to learning. By contrast, the more private form of the home mode typically requires little more than basic "legibility" and hence a much less sustained and systematic approach. These distinctions are of course a question of degree, but they are primarily a function of individuals' needs and motivations. Our participants' activity as video makers depended upon the other social roles they took up, both in their families and in some instances in their working lives. People's motivation to learn, and hence what and how they learn, need to be understood in the context of their broader social practices and identities. For many people, a developed form of media literacy—in the sense of something systematically acquired and theoretically reflected upon—is more or less irrelevant to their needs.

PART 2: LITERACY

Having considered *how* our participants learned about video making, our attention shifts now to look at *what* they learned—that is, the various forms of media literacy they acquired. Our analysis here focuses on several broad themes. First, we look at *the relationship between consumption and production*. How does people's activity as video makers relate to their consumption, particularly of mainstream film and television? To what extent, and in what ways, does consumption inform production; and how does the experience of production feed back into, and potentially change, the nature of consumption? Our second theme is to do with *the "language" of video*. To what extent are our participants aware of the formal or aesthetic aspects of video making, such as camera work and editing? What, if anything, do they learn about these aspects, and how far are they actually relevant for them? Third, we consider the specifically *technological* dimensions of this. How do participants perceive and seek to use the specific "affordances" or potentialities of video as a medium, as compared with other media, such as still photography? Finally, we pick up briefly on a theme that has been raised at several points already, which is the participants' *sense of audience*. To what extent does the existence of a real or hypothetical audience for one's work influence the production process and the extent to which these more formal aspects are addressed?

Here again, there is a degree of diversity. Some participants were quite self-conscious about these issues and talked quite explicitly about the composition and framing of shots, about editing and special effects, or about the role of sound. Others talked about such matters but showed relatively few signs of considering them in what they actually produced. Yet for most participants, most of the time, such issues were really not important at all: what they were interested in was the content. Considerations of aesthetics, form, and "technique" did not matter in their own right, but only in so far as they would allow or impede access to content.

While there were some notable exceptions, few participants related what they did in any sustained way to mainstream media. Home mode video appears to be regarded as a genre in its own right: while it may playfully make use of mainstream media formats, it does not generally aspire to either imitate or challenge them. In general, what our participants valued were the specific possibilities of video as a means of documenting everyday family life, although, as we shall see, they were sometimes ambivalent about its value relative to other media such as still photography. However, this is not to suggest that using video in this way is unproblematic, as we saw in chapter 4. Here again, the *uses* of media literacy depend on how the participants see themselves as video makers and how video making as a practice relates to other social roles they take on in their lives.

From Consumption to Production—and Back Again

Even the most casual form of video making is not a wholly spontaneous or naive practice. Even when deciding where to point the camera and when to press the record button, people are inevitably drawing on some prior knowledge about what a moving image text typically is and how such texts tend to work. We have expectations about what might be interesting for other people (or even just the immediate participants) to watch and what might make it "watchable." While there have been some interesting studies involving video making with people who have no experience of ever watching film or television (Messaris 1994), nearly all home video makers have extensive familiarity with a wide range of moving image media.

In some cases, the relationship between our experience as consumers and producers (or "readers" and "writers") of video is fairly explicit. Throughout our 12 households, there were several examples of videos that referred—either fleetingly or in very overt and sustained ways—to mainstream film and television. These references were sometimes playful and ironic, but also sometimes quite serious and sincere. While there were occasional elements of parody, they hardly ever seemed to be motivated by a desire to critique the values of mainstream media or to "deconstruct" dominant media forms.

Nicole, for example, was involved in rebuilding and decorating a new property and set out to make a video based on the TV makeover show *Property Ladder*, which typically features contrasting "before and after" sequences. Although she recorded various sequences as she went along, actually editing the video remained a potential project for the future—"that would be quite nice to do"—rather than something she actually completed. Similarly, Loren, who was just embarking on what she anticipated would be a lengthy struggle to get rehoused by the Council, set out to make a more personal video diary about the process. Her model here may have been the BBC's *Video Nation* shorts, although she only recalled this as a memory from "a long time ago." While her son Barney found this a little strange—"My mum's a bit weird, 'cause she just talks to the camera"—Loren saw this as a potentially therapeutic process, a matter of creating a personal narrative with a potentially happy ending:

> It helped me to process my thoughts, I suppose. . . . I wanted to film myself at my sort of lowest point, to see, later on, that I'd survived that. I thought that would be a good thing for me. . . . It sort of reminds me that I went through that and I survived, which I might not have felt so conscious of, if I hadn't recorded that at the time.

In the event, Loren's production was also unfinished, as she managed to get rehoused much more quickly than she had anticipated.

Other references to mainstream media were much more fleeting and essentially playful. Phil described his efforts at comedy (as in his rubbish chute video and his videos of pulling grotesque faces to the camera) as being like *Monty Python,* while Neil briefly compared his recordings of his mother and sister arguing to *Big Brother*—although in neither case was there any obvious reference or parallel in the actual videos. However, this playful dimension came through more strongly in the case of some of the children's productions. Barney, for example, produced a brief video of himself and a friend wrestling on the bed in the style of WWE (World Wrestling Entertainment). He also made a couple of videos that seemed to owe something to sadistic game shows: one, which he described as "really nasty," featured him "kidnapping" and blindfolding a friend who was shown stumbling around their flat.

However, the only extended example of this kind of imitation of mainstream media was in Aidan and Ted's family. Ted's videos were described by his mother, Sarah, as a kind of extension of his play as a younger child: "He had *Dumbo* on the video, he'd have to have the train and reenact it, sort of, as it was going on." The children incorporated the video camera in their play, for example, recording themselves playing football and then generating a running commentary as they reviewed it, or using it for "action replays," as Aidan described:

> It's part of that thing of pretending you're in the cup final or playing for England or whatever, that you're playing it and then, "What a goal that was! Let's see the replay!" And then they'll watch it as if they're watching it on TV, and one of them will be doing a commentary. You know, like Max [falling] down, "Oh, what a shock!" They've got all the clichés that the commentators use. Because on their computer games, they have got people impersonating [the commentators] and saying the sort of things they say . . . so they know them all off by heart.

While there may have been an element of parody here, Ted's more elaborate remakes of *Jaws* and the Nike ad, and his projected *Doctor Who* adventure, were much closer to homage than parody and did not seem to be intended satirically—however ludicrous his parents may have found the activity of making them. Ted's Nike ad was partly based on reenacting computer games, but Ted also aimed to incorporate some material recorded from the Nike Web site, including the logo and some short action sequences—thus making this the only example throughout our entire project of the kind of "remix culture" that has been widely discussed in recent years (Ito 2006; Jenkins 2006). Yet at least according to Aidan, the intention here too was very much one of homage rather than critique:

> One of their soccer or football DVD computer games starts off with a kind of montage of famous footballers, you know, a montage of skills where they're flicking the ball up and it's doing this and that to music. And that's what they were trying to emulate, as if it was a Nike ad. . . . They're trying to do a sort of copy of it, not a pastiche for fun; they want it to look serious. But they also want it to look different, not an exact copy. . . . And then I have to sort of lie on the wet Astroturf so the camera is at ball level!

Here, as with the *Jaws* remake, the use of the correct music was also particularly important for Ted, possibly lending his blatantly amateur production a degree of professional authenticity. For Aidan, this kind of amateur video production represented a potential alternative to mainstream TV, which he condemned as "badly written." He referred to some YouTube productions as offering a different model, and he also drew here on the example of his cousin, who had made several Super 8 films in his youth and had "a garage with all the editing equipment and all sorts of nonsense." Yet if Aidan seemed to value Ted's productions as instances of what we might call an alternative amateur aesthetic, he also noted that Ted was a perfectionist, who very much wanted his productions to be like the real thing. Ultimately, though, Aidan's comments about how these projects would be viewed in the future make it clear that they too are essentially a variant of the home mode: the video making is part of the family holiday, the family outing, or the children's play, and it will be remembered as such.

There were a few other instances when participants seemed to be drawing on, or at least referring to, models of video practice that were distinct from the mainstream. Jocelyn talked about the different visual qualities of video and film stock and referred to the Gus Van Sant film *Paranoid Park*, which combines these different formats. Mariya was explicitly critical of dominant media and said she aspired to make videos that were more politically radical (in the mode of citizen journalism) or, alternatively, artistically experimental (she described at one point how interesting it would be to watch a video about the different ways in which water flows). Even so, in neither case was any influence of these apparent alternatives evident in their own productions.

In other instances, different models were somewhat more apparent. The videos Edward made on his travels around London appeared to be intended as travelogues for prospective visitors, although he also referred to the 1960s TV show *Candid Camera* as an example of the kind of unobtrusive filming of people that he was attempting to achieve. As we noted in chapter 3, Bruno's son Klaus developed an interest in animation, largely as a result of being shown this on a school visit, and was beginning to experiment with videotaping short sequences of his toys, often in extreme close-up, although here again, there seemed to be relatively little relationship between this and any television or film animation he had seen.

The examples we have considered here are diverse, and yet in some ways they are all exceptions. For most of our participants, most of the time, the relationship between their own videos and what they saw in mainstream media was simply not an issue. Even for the most enthusiastic and systematic exponents of home mode video making, such as Matt and Yaron, television was something completely different and unrelated. Those who, for different reasons and in different ways, sought to go beyond the private home mode often had only a very vague sense of how this related to media they had experienced as consumers. Aidan and Ted's family represents the only significant instance in our sample of participants using video to rework or remix mainstream media—and in this case, this was essentially a matter of homage rather than critique and an extension of family play rather than a radically new cultural form in the making. Despite the optimistic claims of enthusiasts for "participatory culture" (see chapter 1), none of our participants used the opportunity of video making to challenge or create ideological alternatives to dominant media.

Nevertheless, and perhaps paradoxically, several of them claimed that the experience of production had impacted their media consumption. Making their own videos had led them to watch mainstream film or TV in a different way, they told us: it alerted them to aspects of "film grammar" and the use of particular techniques and artistic effects. These comments were more prevalent among the more self-reflexive of our participants. Jocelyn, for example, said that making videos herself had led her to be more aware of the "technical side" of films:

> Once you understand the technique of something, then you have a greater appreciation of it. But if you have no idea about ballet and you go and watch a ballet, you go [blank face]. But if you take a ballet class and then you go and watch a ballet, and you go, "That's really hard, what they're doing." Because you actually understand the effort, because you've attempted it yourself. So I'm understanding more the technique of it all.

Edward likewise described how his experience of video making had led him to watch television more closely and be more aware of how producers included "little extras to make it more interesting," while Mariya wrote at length in an e-mail to us about how video making had made her more conscious of aspects such as camera angles, lighting, and editing, "the artistic and aesthetic side of a shot":

> I have come to understand that it's a huge art to do it properly and that just an ordinary way of shooting gives you some very ordinary boring image sequence. . . . I think having a camera and using it regularly made me a more educated and appreciative viewer, consumer of image production.

While we might suspect that Mariya is telling us what she believes we want to hear—there is little evidence of this kind of awareness in her actual videos—the educational implications here are nevertheless quite interesting. On one level, making something yourself should help you to understand how the professionals do it—and this assumption is also implicit in the overtly pedagogical approach Aidan adopted with his children, described earlier. Yet, as both the above quotations suggest, this may result in a greater degree of awe and admiration, rather than a more critical approach. As Yaron noted, the more you understand about professional video making, the more daunting and remote it may seem: even short homemade animations on YouTube may take a very long time to create—"It's three weeks' work for a five-minute video—I mean, we [adults] know that, and I think [children] know it." Far from empowering the consumer, the experience of media production might turn out to be positively disillusioning—at least if one expects to be able to create something that in some way resembles mainstream media.

Learning Video Language

Nevertheless, the fact that home mode video makes little reference to mainstream film and television does not mean that it should be seen as a merely spontaneous practice—or indeed a hopelessly naive one. There are numerous instances in our study of participants exercising what might be called a form of artistry—making a deliberate effort to achieve particular aesthetic effects or at least aspiring to do so. This is most immediately evident among those who go beyond the private home mode, although such concerns are also apparent in some of the most limited home mode material.

For example, Aidan and Ted had very definite ideas about the specific composition of shots they wanted to achieve and often went to great lengths to obtain them—including (as we have seen) lying flat on the ground of a wet football pitch and filming underwater in the sea. Ted's episode of *Doctor Who,* for example, involved some complex experimentation with perspective in order to create the illusion of life-size daleks and dinosaurs marauding in the undergrowth at Kew Gardens. Yet this kind of concern with framing and composition was also an issue for Aidan's more conventional home videos: for example, he spoke at length about the difficulty of framing shots when videotaping his daughter Millie's birthday party in their cramped basement flat. Phil appeared to have learned from the example of his brother-in-law, whom he described as "a quite artistic filmmaker": "It's quite interesting how he manages to get . . . very good shots of things that seem very professional, by careful placement of the camera." Although Phil's interests were more in comedy than in what he called "arty" films, he was also concerned about finding the framing and composition that would make for the best effect.

Editing offered further possibilities for some our participants. Jocelyn, for example, was quite clear about the effects she wanted to achieve while editing her Parisian travelogue and talked about "reaction shots" and "drop-ins," while Barney wanted to use editing to create an impression of smoothness and continuity, "to make sure it all fits together . . . to make it work so it looks properly." Both were learning to use editing as a way of constructing narrative and generating rhythm and pace through repetition and cutting on action. Shanta also sought to give narrative shape to her videos and photographic records of her children's performances:

> I actually like to have a beginning, middle and end . . . so before I go to the center where the children are performing, I take a picture of the building and, like, take pictures of the setting and, like, people sitting down . . . and then the end, when they're coming away again.

In some instances, participants were keen to use the possibilities of video to capture mood or "atmosphere." Edward, in particular, enjoyed visual effects such as reflections on windows and blurred lights and also preferred to have natural sound rather than commentary over his London scenes—"I like the sound of what's actually happening. . . . I sometimes think the talking over it is a bit of a nuisance." This kind of documentary naturalism was particularly important for Edward: he was keen on capturing people without them being aware of the camera and also sought to present the perspective of an ordinary visitor to London "just wandering about," rather than a more polished, "professional" view. Yaron—who, like Edward, was a keen amateur photographer—also spoke about the importance of "atmosphere." He too was keen to achieve a sense of "naturalness"—"It's a matter of keeping it authentic . . . a desire to not construct the event to serve the video." Thus, he talked about one of his videos of a family bicycle ride, where the natural sound was particularly important:

> Part of it was, you know, riding along and trying to capture my experience, and there it was interesting because in terms of the sound, it's very serene, there's just the wheels kind of grinding, and birds and water, 'cause we're going along the canal, so that kind of very gentle soundscape was nice.

This issue of naturalism and spontaneity was a particular concern when it came to videotaping family members. Many participants seemed to experience some ambivalence here: they wanted their subjects to behave "normally," as though the camera was not there, and yet they were also interested in getting them to perform. For example, Bruno described the difficulty of getting the younger children in his extended family to "be patient enough to be filmed," while Barney likewise wanted "everything to be natural when the camera's on . . . because if it's not really staged, it works better." Both seemed to agree that video was more effective than still photography in this respect: as Barney put it, "photography is a lot more unreal, 'cause it's all, quite a lot of it is posed." Yaron argued that the large viewfinder on digital cameras was particularly helpful: "You don't have to hold it to your face, so you can look someone in the eye but have the camera shooting at the same time, and I think that's much less intrusive." However, others found this kind of unobtrusive, naturalistic recording rather boring. Both Phil and Matt said they liked to capture their children unawares, but they also said that some of their best material was when the children were deliberately performing for the camera. Thus, Phil set up "games" or "tasks" for his children to perform on camera, while Matt's children acted out short prepared skits. Matt said:

> I actually realized that the most interesting film I've got of them is when they're talking to the camera. So I tried to do more things like that. . . . I'm trying to get more of their personality over, I suppose.

Nevertheless, in the home mode, the issue of "film language"—or even "film art"—is generally a marginal concern. Although our interview questions often focused on such issues, many of our participants were simply not bothered about them. Essentially, they were interested in the content rather than the form, and several of them explicitly said as much. Nicole, for example, said that her motivation for video making was just to do with "keeping memories": she was not concerned about becoming a "good filmmaker." Although she was aware of issues such as composition, all she really wanted to do was to have the subject in the center of the picture and to be able to point and shoot. This was not necessarily a question of technical (in)competence either. Matt, for example, had considerable creative skills in relation to music technology, but was not interested in extending this to his home video making: he saw these as separate activities, with quite distinct functions in his life.

For Mariya, the emotional appeal of the content was such that it would override questions about technique. In this respect, she argued, video was a more effective medium than photography:

> For me, video is a fantastic opportunity to relive the event, with all the emotions of the moment plus the current emotions of nostalgia and retrospective evaluation, and that is something no memory alone or photos can do.

Image quality was important here—Mariya doubted that poor-quality video captured on a mobile phone could carry the same "emotional charge" and said that she found herself "impatient to see the content." Even so, the emotions could be captured and reexperienced relatively easily, without the need to learn elaborate "technique."

Phil, meanwhile, was somewhat critical of what he saw as a tendency for people to show off in their home videos and family photographs. He described a cousin who had made a video of a family trip to America, whose main purpose (according to Phil) was "promoting himself," and he also criticized another relative whose house was full of family images on display:

> I think they want to tell a story about this is what their family's like, so that when someone goes to the toilet in their house, they can see it. It's kind of evidence of . . . whatever they might want to show to people, their success, or values.

However, this is not to imply that he rejected the home mode outright. Indeed, in some respects, Phil appeared to be interested in a more "realistic" representation of family life, which would focus on the more genuinely mundane details of their daily routines, rather than simply on special occasions:

> I just film everyday things. I tend to put [the camera] on randomly. Like when we're having breakfast and arguing about the cereal and stuff like this.

It was these kinds of "ordinary" everyday events and "little details," rather than the special occasions, that Phil argued would be difficult to remember in future and were therefore worth recording. In this sense, he seemed to reject the traditional home mode, not for something more spectacular or unusual, but on the contrary for something more naturalistic and mundane.

The apparent realism of video was valued, therefore, but it was also perceived and defined in different ways. The more dedicated home mode producers in our sample realized that creating a realistic representation was not a spontaneous act, but rather a matter of conscious choice and in some instances of deliberate artifice.

Technology and Literacy

Several of the observations cited above rest on comparisons between video and other media. Most of our participants had experience with several other forms of media production, particularly still photography. Some could recall Super 8 movie film, while many also created video on their mobile phones or on digital still cameras. Their comparisons between these media were partly to do with issues such as portability and ease of use. As we have seen in chapter 3, the domestication of media technology depends to a large extent upon these kinds of logistical considerations. However, our participants also perceived these media as having different expressive or creative possibilities and constraints (or "affordances"): the "language" of video was different from that of still photography or film and therefore required a specific kind of "literacy."

Thus, several participants saw mobile phones as a less obtrusive means of recording fleeting aspects of daily life and hence as permitting a greater degree of naturalism and spontaneity, although the image quality of camcorder video was seen as preferable and as important in terms of prompting memories and emotional responses—as Mikhael put it, "Sometimes you need some good [quality] footage for memories." Similarly, Edward argued that it was possible to capture more of someone's personality with video than with photography and that it was easier to film without people being aware of it. Others valued the ability of video to capture action, particularly in relation to children; its narrative possibilities (or what Bruno called "visual stories"); its ability to capture a sense of space (as when Phil and Bruno used it to film their new houses); and the fact that it did not need as much "explanation" as still photographs, for example.

On the other hand, Neil worried that video was capable of revealing a "secret reality" that was not apparent in still photos and that he would prefer not to be shown: "You can't strike that pose and keep it for the whole time that video is watching you—you kind of have a moment where eventually you're going to slip out of character and you might do something you don't want people to see." (This again reflects Neil's broader concerns about surveillance and disclosure, discussed in chapters 2 and 3.) In a different way, Matt also saw the ease of recording video as a disadvantage: he noted that his father's Super 8 films were significantly more selective (because of the expense), and he was now trying to emulate this in his own video making.

Taken together, these observations suggest that the participants saw these comparisons in terms of a series of "trade-offs" between different criteria. Video obviously had particular affordances, in terms of capturing motion and space and (more nebulously perhaps) in conveying qualities such as character, feeling, and atmosphere. While some found it more obtrusive than a still camera, several argued that it was capable of greater naturalism—although equally for some, that in itself was problematic. Here again, these different valuations reflect the different motivations and circumstances of the participants. The point here is that the physical and technological characteristics of particular media do have implications in terms of their potential for expression or communication and that an awareness of this dimension is one aspect of media literacy more broadly.

The Sense of Audience

The issue of audience has recurred at several points in previous chapters. In chapter 3, we saw how people's apparently "private" video making was located in a broader network of social relationships, both with extended family and friends but also with wider, and potentially unknown, audiences, while in chapter 4, we explored the ways in which the experience of video making can address profound subjective aspects of the relationship between self and other. Here, it is important to note that this sense of a potential or actual audience is a crucial determinant of people's motivation to learn and hence of how and what they learn.

Even those who most enjoyed the activity of video making for its own sake seemed to need a broader motivation for their activity, and this was often provided by having an audience that was wider than just the immediate family. In general, the more concrete and less hypothetical the audience, the more powerful was the motivation it provided. As we have seen, the role of distant family members was often crucial in this respect. Jocelyn, for example, was interested in video making as a creative activity and to some extent as an avenue for future employment, but what motivated her to actually complete her edited travelogue of her trip to Paris was her wish to communicate—at least in the form of a video "postcard"—with her parents in Australia. As for Matt, who wanted to send videos of his children to their grandparents in Ireland, some form of editing was seen as essential in order to render the material "watchable" (or at least less boring) for the audience. Like Matt and Jocelyn, Loren had a family history that involved Super 8 filmmaking, and she too was keen to send videos, in this case of family holidays and the children playing sports, to distant relatives. By contrast, a key motivation for Shanta in videotaping her children's performances was to build up a portfolio that would help her children gain admission to a competitive Islamic private school.

In some instances, the potential audience was somewhat wider. Edward spoke about how the creation of "atmosphere" could help to "capture an audience" and of the need to "tell the story" in a succinct and engaging way: "When I'm taking it, I'm aware that somebody else is going to watch this, and is this interesting for them?" However, when it came to his videos of London, he seemed to have a somewhat hypothetical sense of who this audience might be. At one point, he suggested that American tourists might like to watch his videos—"There's millions of Americans never come here, but they would love to see it." More concretely, he had received some interest in his photography from various sources, as a result of having some of his work published in a local newspaper, and he had also appeared in a film that was shown at County Hall and had been the main subject of a newspaper article about elderly people living in poverty.

Yet across the entire sample, this was one of very few instances of any of our participants having a sustained interest in putting their productions out into the wider public sphere. While some of the "event recordings" were shown to wider audiences (particularly in the context of schools, but also in clubs), in all other cases the audience of family and friends remained the absolute limit of our participants' ambitions. As such, questions about the formal or aesthetic qualities of their video making were bound to remain marginal: like the participants themselves, their audience was likely to be predominantly interested in the content. Some basic media literacy was necessary in order to render videos "watchable": not even the video makers themselves wanted to watch endless amounts of inconsequential raw footage or be distracted by wobbly camera movements, nauseating zooms, or indecipherable soundtracks. But beyond the need to achieve a basic level of coherence and legibility, there was little motivation or interest for most of the participants in developing their creative or technical skills as video makers.

CONCLUSION

Our participants' uses of the camcorder were led by a variety of motivations, which in turn reflected their personal and social circumstances. We have categorized these loosely in terms of the public-private continuum we introduced in chapter 3. In relation to media literacy, practices at the "public" end of this continuum are likely to be much more demanding than those at the "private" end. As such, they are also likely to require a more systematic and reflexive process of learning.

"Private" practices—personal video diaries, recordings of one's children's birthday parties or just of everyday events—are generally intended for an audience that consists of the video maker him- or herself and (often, although not always) close friends or immediate family. As such, it is essentially the content that matters: unless one develops a personal interest in video making for its own sake, nothing much is to be gained from a systematic consideration of "film grammar." Editing is generally unnecessary when one can simply fast-forward or rewind. The more remote the potential audience—for example, in the case of distant family members—the greater is likely to be the incentive to address such matters. Thus, almost all of our examples of editing took place in relation to footage that was intended to be sent to distant family members or friends.

The various forms of "event recording" that exist around the midway point on this continuum are marginally more demanding, in that they require some basic media literacy in order to create something that will be legible or comprehensible to a wider audience. Nevertheless, in practice, the audience here is also likely to be already interested in the content, and the aim is primarily to capture a given event in as comprehensive and undistorted a manner as possible—which would imply that any undue form of "artistry" (or even of editing) might be seen as an unwarranted intervention.

Only when we approach the more "public" end of the continuum do more complex forms of media literacy become necessary. The need to inform and entertain an audience whom one may not know, and who may not be initially interested in the content, requires more by way of advance planning and preparation and greater skill in terms of creating a coherent, succinct, and engaging statement; and this in turn requires a more systematic, reflexive, and "artful" understanding of the medium. Such material is also more likely to be compared with, and conceived in relation to, mainstream media forms and genres.

While some of our participants clearly aspired to move toward this more "public" end of our continuum, in most cases this remained little more than an aspiration—and perhaps one that some of them may have felt obliged to express for our benefit. For most of the time, most participants remained at the "private" end and had little reason to move from there or indeed any great interest in doing so. While some were able to "talk the talk" of media literacy, relatively few were prepared to "walk the walk."

The move along the continuum from private to public is motivated in different ways. It is partly about one's prior experience of creative practice—for example, in the case of our participants who previously had a serious interest in photography or who had a family history of amateur filmmaking. It may also be provoked by an interest in technology in its own right, although this may result in little more than experimentation. More crucially, however, it seems to be motivated by the need or desire to address a wider audience, which itself relates to the wider social context. Our sample is too small to hazard generalizations, but it may be that this has a gender dimension: it was mainly men who sought in various ways to go beyond the most private forms of the home mode (although Jocelyn and Mariya represent exceptions to this).

As we have argued, this is very much a social process. What people learn and how they learn are contingent on their material circumstances and opportunities and on their social motivations, roles, and identities—their sense of who they are or who they would like to become. This analysis points to the need for a *social theory* of media literacy—and in this respect, there are some significant parallels with recent work on print literacy. Sociological and anthropological research has increasingly come to regard literacy as a matter of social practice rather than individual competence and hence as necessarily diverse (Street 2003). A social theory of media literacy would likewise need to acknowledge that "literacies" are plural and that they are defined by the social contexts in which they are used and the social purposes they serve (Buckingham 2003).

Our research suggests that people's acquisition of media literacy is highly contingent on their unique social circumstances and that media literacy is not a set of abstract skills that can be defined in isolation from the settings in which they are acquired and developed. On the contrary, to follow the lead of one of the early pioneers of cultural studies, Richard Hoggart (1957), our focus needs to be on the social *uses* of media literacy. As this implies, we need to know how people's understandings are used in the contexts of everyday practice; but we also need to know what media literacy is used to achieve—what it is good for and why anybody should be motivated enough to want to learn it.

CHAPTER 6

Conclusion

The households we have described in this book were very diverse. They included people from a wide mix of social-class and ethnic backgrounds, and they ranged from large families with young children to a single elderly man living alone. Our participants used their video cameras in some diverse and often surprising ways—not just to record the minutiae of family life but also to rework existing media; to create little dramas, video diaries, and montages; and to play with the possibilities of the medium. In attempting to categorize and analyze this range of uses, we have described a broad continuum from more private to more public practices. On the private end, we have Loren starting her video diary about being rehoused, or Phil pulling faces for the camera; on the more public end, we have Edward's videos of London life, produced for a potential audience of tourists, or Mariya showing her videos to educational policy makers in her home country of Georgia. The material we gathered, or that our participants described, was more diverse than the more predictable forms of family record keeping—the children's birthday parties and family outings—that are typically seen to characterize home video making.

However, it would be misleading to overstate this. Many of the more ambitious or public forms of video production that our participants described remained at the level of aspiration. Many—Ted's remakes, Nicole's property makeover show, Loren's video diary—were unfinished or unedited. In many cases, we were told of videos that were planned (or at least fantasized about) but never made: for example, Neil, Barney, and Phil all hoped to produce music-related videos to upload to video sharing sites, but none of them managed to achieve this. In other instances, we suspect that participants may have been seeking to please us by telling us about more ambitious projects of which we saw very little actual evidence. Even when participants seemed to have extrinsic motivations for video making—for example, their current jobs (as with Bruno) or future career aspirations (as with Jocelyn)—relatively little was actually completed. Even our most dedicated and prolific video maker, Edward, failed to create a finished "production," although he did screen some of his raw footage to his senior citizens' club.

As we have noted throughout, there were significant disparities between people's aspirations regarding video making and the realities of what they actually managed to do. All our participants began with high expectations and with a degree of enthusiasm and excitement. We would accept that this may partly have derived from the fact that they were participating in our research: some of them at least may have wanted to appear as "good research subjects" (which, despite our assurances to the contrary, might have led them to use the camcorder more than they would otherwise have done). Nevertheless, we would argue that this initial enthusiasm would also have been apparent if they had bought the camcorder themselves or been given it as a present. As we saw in chapter 1, the marketing and consumer advice literature that "frames" home video making tends to tell a story of unbridled creativity: it addresses the home video maker as a serious, dedicated hobbyist, rather than a casual or occasional user. The technology is "sold" to consumers on the basis of a certain story about how it will be used and the role it will come to play in their lives: it comes "bundled" or surrounded, not just with useful accessories but also with social, moral, and cultural values (this is the "commodification" phase discussed in chapter 3).

The reality, as many of our participants quite quickly discovered, was rather different from the story. In several cases, the camcorder was used only very rarely or hardly at all: it changed quickly from being an exciting new toy to being merely another element in the detritus of family life. In the event, most of our participants used the camcorder much less, and produced much less, than they had originally hoped. There were several reasons for this. To some extent, this might be put down to difficulties with the technology. Edward, for example, might have engaged in editing if he had been able to do this on his home computer rather than having to go to the local community center. One or two other participants appeared to struggle with operating the camera, albeit only in the early stages of the project; while others were daunted by the prospect of editing. More significant in this respect were the difficulties our participants faced in integrating video making within the routines and daily realities of family life. This was particularly the case for the larger families: Aidan and Ted, for example, were clearly very interested in the creative possibilities of video making, but it was often far from easy to fit this into their busy schedule. In other instances, as with Nicole, events simply took over, which meant that video making had to take a backseat while other problems were dealt with. By contrast, participants with more time on their hands (such as Edward and some of the children) were able to achieve much more.

However, there were more fundamental reasons for this gap between aspiration and reality, having to do with people's motivations and purposes. For various reasons, most of our participants simply did not want or need to create elaborate productions. They did not need to plan out what they were going to do or to edit or engage in complex "postproduction" activities. Their aims were much more modest and mundane. For the most part, they were interested in using video to record and enhance family life, rather than in video making as an end in itself.

As such, it would be wrong to imply that the participants themselves were disappointed with what they managed to achieve. Rather, we would say that they adjusted their expectations in the light of experience. They learned what the camcorder was good for and what it was not so good for. This was partly about the "affordances" of the technology itself and partly about the time that it took to create satisfying products. Thus, Mikhael found that he enjoyed using video to capture intimate family moments, but he came to prefer the more portable and accessible technology of his mobile videophone for this purpose. Yaron spent many hours editing video for distribution to family and friends, but he ultimately came to doubt that this was worth the effort and worried (like many other participants) that it was taking him away from enjoying family life. Jocelyn recognized that video had considerable creative possibilities as a medium, but by the end of the project, she had decided to confine herself to making relatively simple home videos to send to her parents and to concentrate her creative energies elsewhere.

Despite their aspirations, therefore, and despite our earlier comments about the diversity of their practices, most of what our participants videotaped remained firmly within the "home mode." Unwrapping the Christmas presents, blowing out the candles on a birthday cake, going on a family outing to the beach or the children's farm, playing in the park, making dinner with Grandma, clowning around for the camera—these were the kinds of scenes that recurred again and again on the videos we gathered. All would fit very easily within the description of the home mode generated more than twenty years ago by Richard Chalfen (1987). Chalfen's account was primarily based on an analysis of family photography and home movie making, rather than video, yet the continuity here is very striking. As we have noted, James Moran (2002) and others have suggested that video is resulting in a kind of loosening or broadening of the home mode: video's ease of use, and in particular its significantly lower cost, means that a wider range of aspects of family life is being recorded and represented. There may be some truth in this: it is certainly plausible that much *more* footage is being generated even than in the days of Super 8 film cartridges—although few of our participants came anywhere near exhausting the supply of 10 one-hour tapes that we gave them at the start of the project. As we have noted, the material we have gathered is somewhat more diverse than Chalfen's: there is more at the "extremes" of our continuum—both more public material and more private material (see chapter 3). Ultimately, however, we doubt whether most of this material is significantly different in terms of content or form: most of it takes the form of "event recording," most of it focuses on interactions between family members, and much of it takes place on more or less "special" occasions.

The reasons for this have to do not only with technological obstacles or with the logistics of everyday life. Rather, they reflect people's motivations and purposes in video making, which are fundamentally focused on the family and the home. These motivations and purposes obviously vary between different individuals and social groups, and they are bound to change over time—although they may well change at a much slower pace than technology itself. Family life evolves historically in relation to other social changes; and the meanings of "home" are socially and culturally diverse, as numerous sociologists and historians have shown (see, e.g., Lee 2001; Morley 2000; Silva and Smart 1998). Even so, we would suggest that ideas of home and family remain centrally important, even in our apparently fluid, fragmented "late modern" societies; and that home video making can potentially serve significant purposes in terms of representing, exploring, and celebrating these ideas and the emotions that they evoke. In our view, this is not simply a matter of blindly or slavishly reproducing a particular "familial ideology," as critics such as Patricia Zimmerman (1995) have argued. The households in our study (like families in general) were composed in some quite diverse ways, and the idea of "family" was not simply confined to the nuclear family unit or indeed to blood relations.

Furthermore, we would argue that—at least for certain people in certain circumstances—the act of video making can serve important functions in terms of emotion and identity. As we saw in chapter 4, a key motivation for all our participants was the desire to produce a record of their present lives for viewing in the future. They were filming for posterity. As we have noted, very few of them reviewed the videos they had produced: they might screen them shortly after recording, noting some of the mistakes they had made, but they rarely seemed to watch them more than once or twice. However, this does not mean that they would not watch them in future, perhaps several years hence. Indeed, we might even argue that the fact of *having* the recordings—stored perhaps in an old shoe box or in a folder on the home computer—was equally as important as actually *watching* them. Like family photographs, video recordings offer the potential (some might say the fantasy) of assembling a coherent narrative of one's life—a narrative that might provide the sense of consistent identity, of continuity and belonging, that often proves elusive in the ebb and flow of everyday life. While the actual experience of video making, and of appearing on video, was uncomfortable for some, it was worth tolerating because of this: it offered the hope of defeating the passing of time and the anxieties it provoked and of creating future memories that would give meaning to one's life. Like other forms of self-representation such as family photography or diary writing—or indeed blogging or creating a social networking profile—home video making may offer the sense of "ontological security," or coherent subjectivity, that Anthony Giddens (1991) sees as one of the imperatives of modern social life.

In this sense, then, we are seeking to make a case for the home mode and to counter the criticisms of academic and popular commentators who have sought merely to denigrate it. Like Richard Chalfen (1987) and James Moran (2002), we believe that the home mode serves important functions in terms of affirming shared cultural values, establishing a sense of one's place in the world, dealing with the complex emotions that surround the passing of time, and constructing and defining one's own identity. While this is a broadly ideological process, we do not believe it should be seen as inherently or necessarily conservative.

We might go further and seek to affirm the "everyday creativity" or "vernacular creativity" that such practices entail (cf. Willis 1990; Burgess 2006). Home mode video making might even be seen as an instance of the "popular aesthetic" identified by Pierre Bourdieu (1984)—a form of expression that is grounded in everyday lived experience, rather than in the abstract and rarefied domain of high art. However, we do not feel it should be necessary to protest too much in this respect: while there clearly are "creative" and "aesthetic" dimensions to home video making, its fundamental purposes are different from those of "art" (whatever we take that to mean). It is not a form of "naive art," like the work of so-called naive painters. Its meaning derives from the fact that it does not stand apart from life: it is not "special," in the sense that art surely has to be (see Negus and Pickering 2004). On the contrary, its significance derives precisely from its continuity with everyday life—from the very fact that it is mundane, even banal.

It is notable in this respect that what most participants valued about the "affordances" of video as a medium was its potential for spontaneity, for capturing passing feelings and atmospheres, and for naturalism rather than elaborate artifice. By and large, they did not want to make movies or become movie directors: indeed, most of the time, they saw very little relationship between their home videos and the films and television programs they watched. Home video was not seen as a direct challenge to dominant media or a radical new form of popular expression, as some contemporary commentators appear to believe (Hannon et al. 2008). It was something altogether different.

At the same time, some of our participants did engage in more ambitious forms of video production or least talked about doing so. So what motivated this? There were some who clearly found the activity of video making engaging in itself. In several cases, this represented a kind of elaboration of their play, particularly for children but also for some adults: Ted's elaborate film and TV remakes are the obvious example, but we could also cite Phil's quirky comic scenes. Others, like Edward and Mariya, saw themselves as "social record keepers," capturing elements of contemporary social life for others, in other times and places, to watch and possibly learn from.

However, in most cases, the crucial issue here was that of *audience*. In these more ambitious practices, at the more public end of our continuum, video was seen as a means not only of recording, or alternatively of "self-expression," but also of *communication*. It offered the potential of representing aspects of one's own life for others who were, for whatever reason, unable to see or participate in it themselves. This was particularly the case for participants like Jocelyn, Leslie, and Yaron, who had extended family members in distant countries. Here, there was a wish not only to show aspects of their lives but to do so in a form that would be "watchable"—if not positively entertaining, then at least not too boring or too difficult to understand.

Even so, there were few instances of participants wanting to show their work to a wider audience. While some had aspirations in this respect, such as Edward and Mariya, these were only rarely achieved. Some of the most ambitious productions remained confined to friends and family: Ted, for example, was reluctant for us to see his remakes or even to talk about them with us. Furthermore, while the wish to communicate with an audience did motivate some of our participants to develop their media literacy skills—for example, in the case of Jocelyn and Yaron learning to edit—in other cases, this remained relatively limited, mostly because it was seen to be unnecessary. Matt, one of the most effective family video makers among our participants, did some basic editing as he transferred his tapes and (like several others) said he was learning to be more selective in what he shot in the first place. But any more elaborate form of media literacy or technical skill would have been fairly superfluous for him, even though he would certainly have been capable of developing it. Here again, there was a point at which an elaborated form of media literacy might even have undermined the primary aim: for most participants, the premium was on naturalism and spontaneity, rather than on artifice, planning, and deliberation.

Video sharing platforms such as YouTube began to be widely known during the course of our research, and it is interesting to speculate about how far they are likely to change home mode video making in the future. Several of our participants had viewed material on such sites, and some imagined posting on them in the future (particularly those with an interest in making music). It is possible that Edward might have used such sites to distribute his footage of London life (although we suspect he would have wanted some financial return!). In reality, however, Yaron was the only participant who actually did this, and in his case, it is notable that he marked his video as private, restricting access to family and friends. As this implies, it may be that for many people, a *known* audience is much more important in terms of motivation than one that is hitherto unknown. To this extent, we suspect that online video sharing is likely to have more significance for "serious amateurs" who are already quite committed to video making than for ordinary home mode producers (see Buckingham and Willett 2009).

Aspirations regarding the transformative potential of technology—in both academic and popular discourse—rest on an implicitly determinist approach. In the case of video cameras, these particularly focus on the promise of creativity and empowerment: as cameras become more convenient and easier to use, and as editing becomes simpler and more intuitive, so have the barriers to creative expression begun to disappear. We can all be film directors and TV producers now. While we sympathize with such aspirations, our approach in this book has been somewhat more cautious. Technologies clearly do have inherent possibilities and limitations—or "affordances"—although they can also be used in unpredictable ways. Ultimately, however, their effects depend very much on the social contexts in which they are used and the motivations of those who use them.

Video cameras may arrive in people's lives carrying a heavy load of expectations, but as they are gradually incorporated into people's everyday routines, those expectations are inevitably adjusted. Our study provides further evidence that technology does not exert an independent influence on domestic life—nor indeed does it offer much fascination in its own right, at least for most people. It may also be comparatively rare for people to find sufficient motivation in the creative act itself. Some people may discover this or transfer it from other areas, as was the case with Edward, although it may be that, as with Matt and his music making, a developed form of creativity in one area of life is enough and does not necessarily have to translate across into other areas. Some people may be motivated by the desire to communicate—whether with people who are already known in the here and now, with those who are known and yet distant, or with a more hypothetical audience whom they have yet to find. Nevertheless, mere access to equipment does not necessarily guarantee that it will be used, let alone that it will be used critically and creatively. Technology in itself will not make people creative media makers, any more than the widespread availability of pens and paper, or even of the printing press, produced a society of authors.

We would like to conclude with some brief reflections on the research itself. We have been somewhat wary of describing this work as "ethnographic": we did not engage in the kind of long-term observation that we would see as a necessary characteristic of ethnography. However, we deliberately set out to do in-depth, longitudinal, qualitative research. This had several advantages, as well as some limitations. We feel our research has allowed us to get closer to what was really happening in our 12 households than might have been possible, for example, if we had used questionnaires or survey methods. We have been able to "triangulate" among our interviews, our (limited) observations in homes, and the participants' video data, and in the process, we have noted several contradictions between what people say they do and what they are actually doing. Revisiting the households on several occasions also allowed us to understand the processes through which the camcorder was (or was not) integrated in participants' lives over time: we could see the cyclical adjustment of people's expectations, as they discovered what they really wanted to use the technology for and what they did not. All of this has enabled us to gain a sense of what these practices *mean* for the individuals involved and how they fit into the texture of their everyday lives.

If these are the advantages of our approach, one of the most significant disadvantages is to do with our ability to generalize. We have produced what we believe is a rigorous and systematic analysis of what took place in these 12 households, and we hope that this is broadly recognizable to readers in relation to their own experience. Our sample was clearly diverse, in terms of key factors such as gender, social class, ethnicity, and family composition, and it would be reasonable to expect that these things have an influence on how people engage with a practice such as video making. Yet as we have pointed out at various stages, it is almost impossible to generalize about such matters even within our sample, let alone beyond it. The more we read and reread our data, the more we become aware of exceptions to any of the easy or schematic conclusions we might wish to draw.

For instance, there are many more similarities between the middle-class and working-class families in our sample than there are differences. Bruno and Heike may now live in a well-appointed middle-class house, while Matt and Leslie are in a cramped inner London flat, and they may get to visit very different places on their vacations. But the functions of video making in their lives—primarily as a means of recording everyday family life, and particularly their children—are remarkably similar, as indeed are the actual videos they produce. It would be simply false to suggest, for example, that the middle-class families are more likely to orient themselves toward the more "public" end of our continuum, while the working-class ones are more "private," or that the middle-class participants have a more developed or elaborated form of media literacy than their working-class counterparts.

In terms of gender, video appears to be quite ambivalently situated: on one level, it is a technology (and hence a stereotypically male domain), yet on another, it is primarily conceived as a focus for family life and the nurturing of children (a stereotypically female domain). Every generalization that one might wish to identify in this respect is both supported and directly contradicted within our data. We have women who appear frightened of technology, but also men who feel the same way or seem completely indifferent to it (Leslie, Peter). We have both women and men who play the leading role as video makers in their families (Shanta, Nicole, Yaron, Phil). Finally, in terms of age differences, we have quite young children who seemed very engaged by the potential of video making (Klaus) and others of the same age who were not interested in the slightest (Alisa)—as well as some striking differences in this respect between siblings in the same family (Ted and Max, Barney and Joe).

At the same time, the social identities and experiences of our participants obviously did play a significant part in shaping their video making practices or leading them in particular directions. Shanta, the good Muslim mother; Phil, the middle-class bohemian; Edward, the white working-class organic intellectual; Matt, the good father and son; Bruno, the middle-class academic scientist; Neil, the black inner city youth—these are all stereotypes, of course, yet there are strong elements of these social roles that appear in these people's video making practices. As this also implies, there are several variables at stake here—for example, to do with gender, social class, ethnicity, and cultural values—that operate simultaneously. Approaching these social differences via a different research method— a questionnaire survey with a much larger sample, for instance—might enable us to say more definitive things about them, but it would also lose a sense of the complex, interrelated, and highly contextualized ways in which these aspects of social identity are actually lived out.

A final point in relation to research method has to do with our use of the video data themselves. There is certainly a paradox here: although our research is essentially about visual (or audiovisual) practices, our analysis has been based primarily on our participants' words. We have considered the possibility of making some of our video material available online, or even on a DVD attached to this book, but of course this would violate our participants' confidentiality. We have planned to make a short compilation of some of the material (e.g., in order to present at academic conferences); but even if we could satisfy ourselves as regards confidentiality, we suspect that such a production would almost inevitably be unrepresentative. We have felt a nagging guilt throughout this research that we should be "analyzing" our video material in the same systematic way we have analyzed our interview transcripts. But beyond logging and viewing the tapes, and comparing them with the participants' accounts of them, we have been uncertain not just about how to do this (there is no obvious method that we feel would give us purchase on this kind of data) but also about what it might add.

As we have noted, it is not easy to watch other people's home videos, let alone analyze them. In both respects, this is because the material is meaningful to the people involved in a way that it simply is not to us. Even though we do now "know" most of the people contained in these videos, we do not know them at all well or intimately. Furthermore, the meaning of this material is highly specific to a particular time and place: its meaning will change as the participants move on in their lives. Indeed, it is likely that it will become *more* meaningful—or at least more poignant and more emotionally significant—for the participants in the future than it is now, and to this extent, what the individuals say about their videos now is unlikely to account fully for the material's emotional meaning. As we have suggested, the fact of having recorded or captured something or somebody on video may be more significant than the actual video itself— and for most of our participants, it was much more significant than the formal or aesthetic characteristics of the video, which are precisely the aspects that tend to be seized upon in textual analysis.

In approaching this kind of data from the perspective of media and cultural studies, we tend to regard it as a form of "text"—as though we could subject it to the same kind of analysis as we use in deconstructing Hitchcock movies, for example. This is not to say that such an analysis might not be possible or even that our participants' home videos are somehow "unworthy" of it. However, it does rather seem to miss the point. As we have shown, the production of these texts is embedded within the lived realities of people's everyday lives, and it is also part of a much longer process, whereby the present speaks to the future, to a point in time when we know that the meanings of what we watch will have completely changed. Rather than the "text" as a fixed product, it is this *process* that needs to be analyzed, and over the longer term, we suspect this may require new methods of analysis, as well as new theories about culture and communication. While we hope that our research has made a useful contribution to the study of ordinary people's engagements with media and technology, we also hope that it will provide a few pointers toward this broader rethinking of the field.

References

Auchard, E. 2007. Participation on Web 2.0 sites remains weak. Reuters, 17 April. http://www.reuters.com/article/internetNews/idUSN1743638820070418 (accessed 3 December 2007).

Bakardjieva, M. 2006. Domestication running wild: From the moral economy of a household to the mores of a culture. In Berker et al. 2006, 62–79.

Barthes, R. 1984. *Camera lucida.* London: Fontana.

Baum, G. 1991. Private eyes. *Los Angeles Times,* 25 July. http://articles.latimes .com/1991-07-25/news/vw-167_1_home-videos (accessed 21 July 2010).

Beal, S. 2000. *The complete idiot's guide to making home videos.* Indianapolis: Macmillan.

Bennett, J. 2005. *Emphatic vision: Affect, trauma and contemporary art.* Stanford: Stanford University Press.

Berker, T., M. Hartmann, Y. Punie, and K. Ward, eds. 2006. *Domestication of media and technology.* Maidenhead: Open University Press.

Bordwell, M. 1962. *Amateur cinematography.* London: Oldbourne Book Co.

Bourdieu, P. 1984. *Distinction: A social critique of the judgment of taste.* London: Routledge.

Bourdieu, P., with L. Boltanski, R. Castel, J.-C. Chamboredon, and D. Schnapper. 1990. *Photography: A middle-brow art.* Stanford: Stanford University Press.

Buckingham, D. 1996. *Moving images: Understanding children's emotional responses to television.* Manchester: Manchester University Press.

Buckingham, D. 2003. *Media education: Literacy, learning and contemporary culture.* Cambridge: Polity.

Buckingham, D. 2010. Do we really need media education 2.0? Teaching in the age of digital media. In *Digital content creation,* ed. K. Drotner and K. Schrøder. New York: Peter Lang.

Buckingham, D., and S. Bragg. 2004. *Young people, sex and the media.* London: Palgrave.

Buckingham, D., M. Pini, and R. Willett. 2007. "Take back the tube!" The discursive construction of amateur film- and video-making. *Journal of Media Practice* 8 (2): 183–201.

Buckingham, D., and M. Scanlon. 2003. *Education, entertainment and learning in the home.* Buckingham: Open University Press.

Buckingham, D., and J. Sefton-Green. 2003. "Gotta catch 'em all": Structure, agency and pedagogy in children's media culture. *Media, Culture and Society* 25 (3): 379–99.

Buckingham, D., and R. Willett, eds. 2009. *Video cultures: Media technology and amateur creativity.* Basingstoke: Palgrave.

Burgess, J. 2006. Hearing ordinary voices: Cultural studies, vernacular creativity and digital storytelling. *Continuum: Journal of Media and Culture Studies* 20 (2): 201–14.

Burgess, J. 2007. Vernacular creativity and new media. Unpublished doctoral dissertation, Queensland University of Technology, Australia.

Chalfen, R. 1982. Home movies as cultural documents. In *Film/culture: Explorations of cinema in its social context,* ed. S. Thomson, 126–37. Methuen, NJ: Scarecrow.

Chalfen, R. 1987. *Snapshot versions of life.* Bowling Green, OH: Bowling Green State University Press.

Citron, M. 1998. *Home movies and other necessary fictions.* Minneapolis: University of Minnesota Press.

Claparede, E. 1911. La question de la memoire affective. *Archives de Psychologie* 10:361–77.

Clark, J. 2007. *Big dreams, small screens: Online video for public knowledge and action.* Washington, DC: Center for Social Media, American University.

Cleave, A. 1988. *The ABC of video movies: Getting the best from your camcorder.* Manchester, NH: Morgan Press.

Coffield, F. 2000. *The necessity of informal learning.* Bristol: Policy Press.

Consumer Electronics Association. 2006. Digital Camcorders Dominate Analog. http://www.ce.org/Press/CEA_Pubs/2089.asp (accessed 1 May 2008).

Consumer Electronics Association. 2008. Digital America 2008. http://www.ce.org/Press/CEA_Pubs/1964.asp (accessed 8 May 2008).

Derrida, J. 1988. On the deaths of Roland Barthes. In *Philosophy and non-philosophy since Merleau-Ponty,* ed. H. J. Silverman, 259–96. London: Routledge.

Dovey, J. 2000. *Freakshow: First person media and factual television.* London: Pluto.

Finnegan, R. 1998. *Tales of the city: A study of narrative and urban life.* Cambridge: Cambridge University Press.

Fiske, J. 1987. *Television culture.* London: Methuen.

Fraser, N. 1992. Rethinking the public sphere: A contribution to the critique of actually existing democracy. In *Habermas and the public sphere,* ed. C. Calhoun, 109–42. Cambridge, MA: MIT Press.

Geist, M. 2006. The rise of clip culture online. BBCNews, 20 March. http://news
.bbc.co.uk/1/hi/technology/4825140.stm (accessed July 2007).

Giddens, A. 1991. *Modernity and self-identity*. Cambridge: Polity.

Gray, A. 1992. *Video playtime: The gendering of a leisure technology*. London:
Routledge.

Haddon, L. 2004. *Information and communication technologies in everyday life*.
Oxford: Berg.

Hall, S. 1996. Introduction: Who needs "identity"? In *The question of cultural
identity*, ed. S. Hall and P. du Gay, 3–17. London: Sage.

Hannon, C., P. Bradwell, and C. Tims. 2008. *Video republic*. London: Demos.

Hirsch, M. 1997. *Family frames: Photography, narrative and postmemory*. Cambridge, MA: Harvard University Press.

Hirsch, M. 2003. I took pictures: September 2001 and beyond. In *Trauma at
home after 9/11*, ed. J. Greenberg, 69–87. London: University of Nebraska
Press.

Hi-Spek Electronics. 1988. Advertisement. *Camcorder User* 1:34.

Hoggart, R. 1957. *The uses of literacy*. London: Chatto and Windus.

Holland, P. 1991. History, memory and the family album. In Spence and Holland
1991, 1–14.

Hoover, S., L. Schofield Clark, and D. Alters. 2004. *Media, home and family*.
New York: Routledge.

Islington Council. N.d. http://www.islington.gov.uk/Environment/Planning/
MajorSchemes/KingsCross/ (accessed 16 July 2008).

Ito, M. 2006. Japanese media mixes and amateur cultural exchange. In *Digital
generations: Young people and new media*, ed. D. Buckingham and R. Willett, 49–66. Mahwah, NJ: Erlbaum.

Jameson, F. 1991. Video: Surrealism without the unconscious. In *Postmodern-
ism; or, The cultural logic of late capitalism*, 67–96. Durham, NC: Duke
University Press.

Jenkins, H. 1992. *Textual poachers: Television fans and participatory culture*.
London: Routledge.

Jenkins, H. 2006. *Convergence culture: Where old and new media collide*. New
York: New York University Press.

Jenkins, H., with K. Clinton, R. Purushotma, A. J. Robison, and M. Weigel.
2006. *Confronting the challenges of participatory culture: Media education
for the twenty-first century*. MacArthur Foundation. http://www.digitallearn
ing.macfound.org (accessed 27 November 2007).

Keen, A. 2007. *The cult of the amateur*. London: Nicholas Brealey.

Kodak. 1966. *How to make good home movies*. New York: Kodak Publications.

Kuhn, A. 1995. *Family secrets: Acts of memory and imagination*. London:
Verso.

LabGuy's World. N.d. Museum of extinct video cameras. http://www.lab guysworld.com/VTR-Museum_002.htm (accessed 8 May 2008).

Lacan, J. 1968. The mirror-phase as formative of the function of the I. *New Left Review* 51:71–77.

Lally, E. 2002. *At home with computers*. Oxford: Berg.

Lee, N. 2001. *Childhood and society*. Buckingham: Open University Press.

Lull, J. 1990. *Inside family viewing*. London: Sage.

Market Wire. 2005. YouTube receives $3.5M in funding from Sequoia Capital: Internet commerce pioneers from PayPal reunite to make videos fast, fun and easy for consumers to create their own personal video network. http://www .marketwire.com/mw/release.do?id=736129&sourceType=1 (accessed 8 May 2008).

Martin, R. 1991. Unwind the ties that bind. In Spence and Holland 1991, 209–21.

McRobbie, A. 1978. Working class girls and the culture of adolescent femininity. In *Centre for contemporary cultural studies: Women take issue*, 96–108. London: Hutchinson.

Messaris, P. 1994. *Visual "literacy": Image, mind and reality*. Boulder, CO: Westview.

Miller, D. 1998. *A theory of shopping*. Cambridge: Polity.

Miller, D. 2008. *The comfort of things*. Cambridge: Polity.

Mintel. 2008. Britain develops into a nation of budding Spielbergs. http://www .marketresearchworld.net/index.php?option=com_content&task=view&id= 557&Itemid=48 (accessed 16 July 2008).

Moran, J. 2002. *There's no place like home video*. Minneapolis: University of Minnesota Press.

Morley, D. 1986. *Family television*. London: Comedia.

Morley, D. 1992. *Television, audiences and cultural studies*. London: Routledge.

Morley, D. 2000. *Home territories: Media, mobility and identity*. London and New York: Routledge.

Negus, K., and M. Pickering. 2004. *Creativity, communication and cultural value*. London: Sage.

Norris Nicholson, H. 1997. In amateur hands: Framing time and space in home-movies. *History Workshop Journal* 43:198–213.

Norris Nicholson, H. 2001. Seeing how it was? Childhood geographies and memories in home movies. *Area* 33 (2): 128–40.

Ofcom. 2004. *What is media literacy?* http://www.ofcom.org.uk (accessed November 2008).

Ouellette, L. 1995. Camcorder dos and don'ts: Popular discourses on amateur video and participatory television. *Velvet Light Trap* 36:33–44.

Pini, M. 2009. Inside the home mode. In Buckingham and Willett 2009, 172–90.

PMA Foresight. 2008. Data watch: Differences in usage and printing by resolution of camera phones. http://pmaforesight.com/2008/04/28/data-watch-differences-in-usage-and-printing-by-resolution-of-camera-phones.aspx (accessed 8 May 2008).

Reay, D. 1996. Dealing with difficult differences: Reflexivity and social class in feminist research. *Feminism and Psychology* 6 (3): 443–56.

Rose, G. 2003. Family photographs and domestic spacings: A case study. *Transactions of the Institute of British Geographers* 28 (1): 5–18.

Sefton-Green, J. 2004. *Literature review in informal learning with Technology Outside School.* Bristol: NESTA Futurelab.

Silva, E., and C. Smart, eds. 1998. *The new family?* London: Sage.

Silverman, D. 2004. *Qualitative research: Theory, method and practice.* London: Sage.

Silverstone, R. 2006. Domesticating domestication: Reflections on the life of a concept. In Berker et al. 2006, 229–48.

Silverstone, R., and E. Hirsch, eds. 1992. *Consuming technologies: Media and information in domestic spaces.* London: Routledge.

Silverstone, R., E. Hirsch, and D. Morley. 1992. Information and communication technologies and the moral economy of the household. In *Consuming technologies: Media and information in domestic spaces,* ed. R. Silverstone and E. Hirsch, 15–31. London: Routledge.

Slater, D. 1991. Consuming Kodak. In Spence and Holland 1991, 49–59.

Slater, D. 1995. Domestic photography and digital culture. In *The photographic image in digital culture,* ed. M. Lister, 129–46. London: Routledge.

SMECC (Southwest Museum of Engineering, Communications and Computation). N.d. DVK-2400 product literature. http://www.smecc.org/sony_cv_series_video.htm (accessed 8 May 2008).

Sontag, S. 1977. *On photography.* London: Penguin.

Sony Electronics. 2007. Why choose Sony Handycam® camcorders? http://www.sonystyle.com/is-bin/INTERSHOP.enfinity/eCS/Store/en/-/USD/SY_ViewStatic-Start?page=static%2farticles%2fhandycamguide%2eisml) (accessed 29 March 2007).

Spence, J. 1986. *Putting myself in the picture.* London: Camden Press.

Spence, J. 1991. Shame-work: Thoughts on family snaps and fractured identities. In Spence and Holland 1991, 226–36.

Spence, J. 1995. *Cultural sniping: The art of transgression.* New York: Routledge.

Spence, J., and P. Holland, eds. 1991. *Family snaps: The meanings of domestic photography.* London: Virago.

Stebbins, R. 2007. *Serious leisure.* New Brunswick, NJ: Transaction.

Steedman, C. 1986. *Landscape for a good woman.* London: Virago.

Stone, M., and D. Streible, eds. 2003. *Small-gauge and amateur film.* Special issue of *Film History: An International Journal* 15 (2).

Street, B. 2003. What's "new" in new literacy studies? Critical approaches to literacy in theory and practice. *Current Issues in Comparative Education* 5 (2): 77–91.

Total Rewind. N.d. Sony BMC-100. http://www.totalrewind.org/cameras/C_BMC1.htm (accessed 8 May 2008).

van Dijck, J. 2005. Capturing the family: Home video in the age of digital reproduction. In *Shooting the family: Transnational media and intercultural values*, ed. P. Pisters and W. Straat, 25–40. Amsterdam: Amsterdam University Press.

Walkerdine, V. 1986. Video replay: Families, films and fantasy. In *Formations of fantasy*, ed. V. Burgin, J. Donald, and C. Kaplan, 167–99. London: Routledge.

Walkerdine, V. 1990. *Schoolgirl fictions*. London: Verso.

Walkerdine, V., and H. Lucey. 1989. *Democracy in the kitchen: Regulating mothers and socialising daughters*. London: Virago.

Wallman, S. 1984. *Eight London households*. London: Tavistock.

Ward, K. 2006. The bald guy just ate an orange: Domestication, work and home. In Berker et al. 2006, 145–64.

Willett, R. 2009. Always on: Camera phones, video production and identity. In Buckingham and Willett 2009, 210–29.

Willis, P. 1990. *Common culture: Symbolic work at play in the everyday cultures of the young*. Milton Keynes: Open University Press.

Yen, Yi-Wyn. 2008. YouTube looks for the money clip. CNNmoney.com, 25 March. http://techland.blogs.fortune.cnn.com/2008/03/25/youtube-looks-for-the-money-clip/ (accessed 8 May 2008).

Zimmerman, P. 1995. *Reel families: A social history of amateur film*. Indianapolis: Indiana University Press.

Index

access to media production technologies, 1, 5, 18, 24–26, 107–8, 150
aesthetics of home video, 14, 131–32, 139, 147, 153
affordances of camcorders, 78, 109, 125, 136–37, 144, 147, 149
amateur movie making, 1, 12–17
America's Funniest Home Videos, 7, 24
artistic expression, 14, 26, 28, 70, 121, 123, 130–32. *See also* creativity
audience, 25, 51, 53–54, 56–57, 65, 74–76, 78, 80, 84, 108–10, 115, 125–26, 137–42, 148–50
authenticity, 20, 91, 129. *See also* realism

Barthes, R., 22, 95, 104
Big Brother, 128
Bourdieu, P., 21–23, 147
Buckingham, D., 2, 3, 12, 24, 26, 29, 30, 108, 141, 149
Burgess, J., 3, 18, 26, 147

cell phones. *See* mobile phones
Chalfen, R., 2, 10, 15–17, 22, 52–55, 64, 67, 70–72, 78, 80, 94, 101–3, 145, 147
Citron, M., 22
Claparede, E., 94, 105
class, social, 22–23, 33, 151–52
"convergence culture," 3, 24
creativity, 14–15, 17, 49, 62, 70–73, 80, 84, 108–9, 122–23, 138–40, 143–44, 149–50
  everyday or vernacular, 26, 147
cultural capital, 26, 57

democratization of media, 3, 18–28, 132, 149. *See also* "convergence culture"; participatory culture
Doctor Who, 34, 72, 128, 132
domestication of technology, 15, 17, 23–24, 30, 48–56, 136
Dovey, J., 27

editing video, 14, 56, 59, 72, 79, 99–100, 113–18, 132–33, 139–40, 144
emotions, 85–106, 123, 135, 147
empowerment. *See* democratization of media

family, representation of, 1, 18–23, 79, 96–98, 135–36, 145–46. *See also* narrative
fantasy, 21, 50, 62, 82–83, 98–101, 106
film grammar or language, 14, 65, 108–10, 131–36, 139
Finnegan, R., 30

gender, 60, 65, 89, 117, 121, 141, 151–52
Giddens, A., 27, 56–57, 147
Gray, A., 30, 51, 121

Haddon, L., 15, 48, 51
Hirsch, E., 15, 48, 50, 52, 80
Hirsch, M., 22, 98, 103
Holland, P., 21, 97
"home mode" video, definition of, 2, 16, 20, 54. *See also* Chalfen, R.
home video making
  ambitions and expectations in relation to, 54–58, 61, 71, 110, 123, 139–40, 143–44, 149–50